NO MEAT FOR ME, PLEASE!

Recipes For The Vegetarian In The Family

D0774115

NO MEAT FOR ME, PLEASE!

Recipes For The Vegetarian In The Family

by

Jan Arkless

PAPERFRONTS
ELLIOT RIGHT WAY BOOKS,
KINGSWOOD, SURREY, U.K.

Typeset in 10pt Times by EMS Photosetters, Rochford, Essex

Made and Printed in Great Britain by Richard Clay Ltd., Bungay, Suffolk.

CONTENTS

With much love to Annabel and Nikki,
have fun on your African adventures,
enjoy your cooking and come home
safely.

P.S. They did.

INTRODUCTION

You realise that things are getting serious when your newly-announced vegetarian always seems to be mysteriously hanging about in the kitchen on a Sunday, just when it's time to put the roast potatoes into the oven, trying to make sure that they are not put into the tin with the meat, and then re-appearing when it's time to make the gravy. We now have a "special vege-gravy jug" in our house. It deliberately doesn't match the rest of the dinner service to make it easier for the rest of us who might absentmindedly help ourselves from it, to a howl of protest from our vegetarian!

When it first became apparent that my daughter was stopping eating meat, I discovered that I really knew very little about vegetarianism. My only contact with vegetarian meals had been at school dinners, where vegetarians were served the same as the rest of us, apart from the fact that the slice of meat was replaced by a square of cheese, often smothered in gravy. It got a bit complicated when we had shepherd's pie or stew. I'm not sure what happened then! Years later, we went on holiday to a villa in Spain, accompanied by a friend of my daughter, who casually mentioned that she was vegetarian, but didn't eat cheese as it gave her migraine. She insisted that at home her Mum didn't cook her anything special, she just ate the family meals without the meat, and she certainly looked a picture of health. I salved my conscience with the thought that it was only for a fortnight, and I don't suppose anyone would suffer from serious malnutrition just for that time, on a diet of mushroom pizza and chips, supplemented with fizzy drinks consumed at the beach cafés, which both girls enjoyed whenever possible!

However, a few months later when it became apparent that my daughter was even refusing her favourite lemon chicken dish, I started to investigate vegetarian cooking seriously, and what an interesting and rewarding experience that has proved to be! Instead of boring old meat and two veg, we have experimented with lots of different vegetarian dishes, and found that if you serve several kinds of vegetables it provides such a satisfying meal that you don't notice the lack of meat.

Vegetarian meals are just a different way of cooking and eating, which may seem strange at first, but soon becomes easy and everyday. Start off slowly, using familiar ingredients and dishes – vegetable flans, cheese and egg dishes, and more substantial dishes like crispy cabbage casserole, which can be eaten on their own or padded out with a filled jacket potato to satisfy healthy appetites. Don't be scared by the vision of "the vegetarian", dressed in compulsory dirndl skirt or baggy trousers with flat open sandals, forever boiling up great steaming pans of beans and lentils to eat out of wooden bowls with home-made wholemeal bread. It doesn't have to be like that!

We have had great fun experimenting with different dishes and finding completely new ingredients which I have never cooked before. The shelves of our village Good Food shop proved to be stacked with all kinds of packets of easy-to-prepare vegetarian dishes which we got used to first, before embarking on recipes using all the dried beans, peas and lentils, lots of different nuts, seeds and spices, wholemeal pasta, brown rice etc., also available in the shop. We always seemed to be making breadcrumbs or grating nuts, lots of our favourite recipes include these (granary bread makes lovely crunchy crumbs). So if possible it is wise to invest in a food processor or liquidiser if you don't already own one. I started taking a greater interest in the vast range of hard and soft cheeses, cottage cheeses, yoghurts and the fresh vegetables, both familiar and unusual, now available in the local supermarket. One always seems to be finding new ways of adding a little extra nutrition to the vegetarian diet – add an egg to this, a handful of nuts to that, grate a bit of cheese on top, stir in half a teaspoonful of vegetable extract and serve an accompanying green salad with lots of raw vegetables whenever possible. The possibilities are endless, and Mum becomes very adept at adding these extras when needed without anyone knowing – what the eye doesn't see, the heart doesn't grieve . . . !

There are lots of individual chilled and frozen vegetarian dishes available in the supermarkets, ranging from the exotic (spicy aubergine savoury) to the more humble vegeburger. Some can be a bit expensive but they are a very useful standby, particularly if you have a freezer and can keep one or two dishes ready in reserve for emergencies for quickly cooked "instant" meals. A microwave oven is an invaluable asset when defrosting and reheating meals for one; both the commercially prepared dishes and single portions of home cooked food, prepared and frozen earlier, are ready to eat in a few minutes.

I have gradually found that it is very easy to prepare general family meals and special vege meals together – casseroles use the same basic vegetables, just cook them in two different pans using different spoons, adding meat to one lot and beans to the other. Lasagne, bolognese, stroganoff, even pasties and lots of other dishes can be prepared together. T.S.P. (Textured Soya Protein) can be a useful addition to the vegetarian diet ("but not too often please Mum" I hear the cry.) It is available in different forms, including mince and chunks, and when prepared correctly it closely resembles meat in looks and texture, but with the virtue of having no animal connections, and it's no problem to prepare "in tandem" with similar meat dishes.

The vegetarian dish, e.g. Italian courgettes, can sometimes serve the whole family, providing the main meal for a vegetarian with an average appetite, and can be padded out with a filled jacket potato for a hungry vegetarian or served with meat or fish for the rest of the family. Many vegetarian dishes can be enjoyed by everyone, especially now the general trend is towards eating less meat both on health as well as moral grounds. Flans, omelettes, other egg, cheese and vegetable dishes are now popular and acceptable to both meat eaters and all except the most extreme vegetarians alike, and once non-vegetarians have been persuaded to try some of the delicious "real" vegetarian dishes I think many people will be pleasantly surprised. We've not found anyone who didn't like nut roast when eventually persuaded to try it. Although not wanting to give up eating meat, they may enjoy the occasional vegetarian meal as a pleasant change.

If served in suitable size portions, lots of the dishes can make a good main meal, a starter, a light lunch, or a supper. Some of the dishes in Chapter 4 also make good lunches or suppers if served in slightly larger quantities.

GLOSSARY, ABBREVIATIONS AND MEASUREMENTS

Some of the cooking terms used in this book which may be unfamiliar to the less experienced cook:-

Al dente — referring to pasta or rice that is cooked and feels firm when bitten.

Baking — cooking food in the oven.

Beating — mixing food with a whisk, wooden spoon or fork so that any lumps disappear and it becomes smooth.

Binding — adding eggs, cream or liquid to a dry mixture to hold it together.

Blending — mixing a dry ingredient (i.e. flour or cornflour) with a little liquid to make a smooth, runny, lump-free mixture.

Boiling	– cooking food in boiling water (i.e. at a temperature of 100°C/212°F) with the water bubbling gently.
Browning	– cooking food in a hot oven or under a hot grill for a few minutes to colour the top.
Casserole	– an oven-proof or flame-proof dish with a lid; also a stew cooked in the oven.
Chilling	– cooling food in a fridge without freezing.
Colander	– a perforated metal or plastic basket used for straining and draining food.
Deep-frying	– immersing food in hot, deep oil and frying it – *do please use a proper deep fat fryer!*
Dicing	– cutting food into small cubes.
Dot with butter	– cover food with small flakes or pieces of butter.
Frying	– cooking food in a little oil or butter in a pan (either a flat frying pan or saucepan).
Greasing	– rubbing fat over a cooking container so that food doesn't stick to it.
Grilling	– cooking food by direct heat under a grill.
Mixing	– combining ingredients by stirring.
Poaching	– cooking food in very gently simmering water, which is just below boiling point.
Purée	– food passed through a sieve, processor or liquidiser, and reduced to a pulp.
Roasting	– cooking food in a hot oven, usually with a little hot oil.
Sautéing	– frying food quickly in hot, shallow fat and turning it frequently in the pan so that it browns evenly on all sides.

Seasoning   – adding salt, herbs and spices to food.
Simmering   – cooking food in water or sauce which is
              just below boiling point, so that only an
              occasional bubble appears.
Straining   – separating solid food from liquid by
              draining it through a sieve or colander.

Abbreviations and Measurements used in this book

The ingredients mentioned in the recipes should all be readily available at most supermarkets as well as specialist health food shops, so there should be no need to search for them.

Measurements are given in both imperial and metric (this should make life easier for all generations of cooks!) but do not combine the two as quantities may not be exact conversions.

In case you don't have kitchen scales, or find it more convenient, I have included some measurements in spoonfuls and teacups (normal drinking size) when possible. I have used size 2–3 eggs in the recipes as these are the ones I usually have in stock.

In the recipes:
tsp   = teaspoon
tblsp   = tablespoon (serving spoon)
1 spoonful   = 1 slightly rounded spoonful
1 level spoonful   = 1 flat spoonful
1 cupful   = 1 teacup size (drinking size cup),
                       approximately ¼ pt/5 fluid oz/142ml

Do not confuse this with the American measure which is 8 fluid oz and is not used in this book.

You may find the following measurements useful:

Beans (including peas and lentils)

DRIED	– 1 heaped tblsp dried beans	= 1 oz/25g
	½ cup dried beans	= 3 oz/75g
	6 oz/150g/1 cup dried beans	= 1 x 15 oz/435g can beans

COOKED	– 2 tblsp cooked beans	= 1 oz/25g
	1 cup cooked beans	= 6 oz/150g
	12 oz/300g/2 cups cooked beans	= 1 x 15 oz/435g can beans

Breadcrumbs

| | 4 heaped tblsp | = 1 oz/25g |
| | 1 not-quite-full-cup | = 1 oz/25g |

(breadcrumbs seem to make a huge volume for their weight).

Butter, margarine

1 inch/2½cm cube = 1 oz/25g. It is easy to divide up a new packet and mark it out into 8 or 10 squares.

Cheese

1 inch/2½cm cube = 1 oz/25g approximately.

Flour, cornflour

1 very heaped tblsp = 1 oz/25g approximately.

Garlic

1 clove fresh garlic means 1 segment, not the whole bulb!!

Nuts

1 heaped tblsp shelled or chopped nuts = 1 oz/25g approximately

1 very full cup shelled or chopped nuts = 4 oz/100g approximately

Pasta – wholemeal or white, shells, etc
1 very full cup dry pasta = 3 oz/75g approximately

Rice – brown or white
½ cup dry uncooked rice = 2 oz/50g approximately
2 cups cooked rice = 4 oz/100g approximately

MISCELLANEOUS HINTS

Beans: when cooking a meal for one, or if you only need a small amount, it's easier to use a can of beans, or to cook a larger quantity of dried beans and freeze individual servings (about 1 cupful) for use later. I find those little plastic containers with lids are just right for keeping in the freezer. If you need a larger quantity it's easy to defrost two or more pot fulls, but it's rather difficult to try and chip a corner off a large block. Dried beans will keep for up to a year (check the date on the packet when you buy them) and I usually decant them from the packets into large screw-top jars (clean empty coffee jars) to help keep them fresh and to stop them from spilling all over the cupboard.

Breadcrumbs: brown or white bread is interchangeable in all the recipes, but I prefer the lovely crunchy breadcrumbs made from granary bread. Crumble the bread in a processor or liquidiser if possible, it's much easier on the fingers than grating by hand! Breadcrumbs will keep for a few days in the fridge in a covered bowl, or can be frozen in portions in plastic bags in the freezer, so it makes sense to prepare a larger quantity when using the processor or liquidiser.

Herbs: chop small quantities of fresh herbs by washing the sprigs or leaves, and then snipping finely with kitchen scissors. It's quicker than chopping with a knife on a chopping board. If you have a glut of fresh herbs in the garden and would like to preserve some to see you through the coming winter, wash and dry them thoroughly (pat gently in kitchen paper), then chop or scissor-snip into small plastic tubs and freeze. Provided the herbs are dry when frozen, they will stay separate and can be scooped out with a teaspoon as needed.

Nuts: chop in a processor, liquidiser or mouli-type grater but be careful not to reduce them too finely. "Rough chop" small quantities with sharp kitchen scissors. Decant large packets of nuts into screw-top jars and store small packets together in a plastic box (clean empty ice-cream tub).

Ketchup: a dollop of ketchup (tomato, mushroom or otherwise) or various commercial sauces, gives flavour to gravies, sauces and stews (and so does a slurp of sherry or wine!). Tomato ketchup can be used as a substitute for tomato purée.

Frozen food: if you have use of a freezer, make double helpings of individual vegetarian meals when possible, and freeze one portion to save time and effort another day. Small foil dishes or microwave plastic dishes, according to how you intend to defrost them later, are suitable for this. If possible, defrost home prepared frozen dishes before cooking or reheating them, it's easier to heat them right through then. I prefer to freeze most home-made vegetarian meals uncooked (i.e. nut roasts) then they don't get too dry on reheating, and I try to leave stews, casseroles and "saucy" dishes undercooked, so that the final cooking can take place during the reheating. Always make sure reheated food is cooked right through not just warmed, as otherwise it can make you ill. If cooking commercially frozen dishes, follow the manufacturer's instructions.

Containers: small foil containers, or dishes sold for use in the microwave, are handy for storing and cooking individual meals. If defrosting in the microwave but cooking convention-ally, I decant the frozen food from a foil dish into an oven-proof dish which can be used in both types of oven. I'm a real miser and wash and re-use these types of dishes. I also save the plastic containers with lids, which have previously contained yoghurt, cream, cottage cheese, coleslaw etc. from the delicatessen counter, as they are very useful for storing portions of home-made sauces and gravies.

STARTERS, SNACKS AND SALADS

A lot of these dishes are interchangeable, they can be eaten as a starter, a snack or an accompaniment, according to the size of portion, appetite and the way in which they are presented.

CURRIED MILLET

Serves 2–4

This makes a nice soft "pâté" which can be eaten with toast and salad as a starter, lunch or supper dish. It will keep like pâté, covered with clingfilm in the fridge.

Preparation and cooking time: 35–40 minutes.

4 oz/100g/¾ cup millet
½ pt/284ml/2 cups hot water
½ tsp mild curry powder   *(continued overleaf)*

(Curried Millet continued)

**1 tblsp roughly chopped mixed nuts
or 1 tblsp coconut
1 tblsp raisins
Salt, pepper
1 orange – peeled and sliced – for decoration**

Put millet in a sieve and rinse thoroughly. Tip it into a saucepan, cover with 2 cups hot water and stir over a moderate heat until it comes to the boil. Reduce heat and simmer with the lid on, for 25–30 minutes, stirring occasionally, until all the water is absorbed. Remove from heat.

Mix curry powder, nuts or coconut, and raisins and stir into millet. Season to taste with salt and pepper. Put into a serving dish and decorate with orange slices.

BAKED AVOCADO   *Serves 1*

Sprinkle the spare half of the avocado with lemon juice to stop it browning, wrap it in plastic film and store it in the fridge for tomorrow's lunch. Leave the stone in; the pear will keep better.

Preparation and cooking time: 20–25 minutes.

½ large, ripe avocado pear
1 tsp lemon juice
1 oz/25g Cheddar or Edam cheese
Few sprigs of fresh chives or 1–2 spring onions
Few sprigs of fresh parsley

1 heaped tblsp pine kernels or chopped walnuts, pecan nuts or
hazel nuts
2 tsp canned or cooked sweetcorn
1 tblsp white wine or cider
Salt, pepper
Cayenne or paprika pepper

Heat oven – 200°C/400°F/gas 6–7.

Cut avocado in half, and place on a lightly greased oven-
proof dish. Sprinkle cut surfaces of avocado with lemon
juice to stop browning, and store the spare half as above.

Grate cheese into a small basin, wash chives and scissor-
snip into grated cheese, or wash and trim spring onion (trim
off roots and yellow leaves, but retain as much of the green as
looks appetising) and chop or snip onion into the cheese.

Wash and scissor-snip parsley into the cheese mixture.
Add pine kernels or chopped nuts and sweetcorn, and mix
together with wine or cider. Season with salt, pepper and a
little lemon juice to taste.

Pile mixture into the avocado – it will heap up on top of
the pear.

Bake in the hot oven for 10–15 minutes until golden brown
and bubbling.

Serve with crispy bread rolls or hot garlic bread.

GRILLED AVOCADO SNACK   *Serves 1*

Quick and tasty and a change from cold avocado.

Preparation and cooking time: 10 minutes.

1 length of French bread (according to appetite)
Butter for spreading
½ avocado pear
1 oz/25g cheese
½ tblsp chopped walnuts

Slice French bread in half lengthways, and spread with butter.

Peel avocado pear and slice it lengthways. Grate or thinly slice cheese.

Arrange layers of avocado on the bread, top with grated cheese or cheese slices, and sprinkle with chopped walnuts (press them down well to stop them sliding off).

Toast under a hot grill for a few minutes until golden, bubbly and melting.

Eat at once.

GARLIC MUSHROOMS   *1 generous serving*

Delicious, but try to persuade the whole family to have some as the garlic is quite potent. The non-converted can make a more substantial meal by the addition of fried or grilled bacon.

Preparation and cooking time: 10 minutes.

3–4 oz/75–100g mushrooms
1–2 cloves garlic or ¼ tsp garlic powder or paste
1 oz/25g butter with 1 tsp vegetable oil
2 thick slices of bread – granary is nice

Wash mushrooms, slice thickly if very large.

Peel and crush fresh garlic.

Melt butter and oil in a saucepan over a moderate heat.
Add garlic and mix well, then stir in mushrooms and fry
gently for 3–5 minutes, stirring and spooning the garlic-
flavoured-butter over the mushrooms.

While mushrooms are cooking, toast the bread lightly, cut
in half and put onto a hot plate. Spoon mushrooms onto the
toast, pour any remaining garlic butter over the top.

Eat at once, lovely!

BLUE CHEESE PÂTÉ   *Serves 2*

Make a pâté with the cheese of your choice, Stilton, Danish
Blue, Gorgonzola, Rocquefort, etc. Use curd cheese in
preference to full fat soft cheese if you are counting the
calories. This makes a useful starter, as it can be made in
advance and frozen or stored in the fridge until needed.
Good for a quick lunch or supper time snack.

*Preparation time: 10 minutes, plus at least 30 minutes standing
time.*

3 oz/75g blue cheese
4 oz/100g curd cheese or full fat cream cheese
1 tblsp milk
1tblsp dry white wine or cider
Salt, pepper

Garnish
Fresh fruit – grapes, apples, pears, nectarines or peaches
Walnut halves
Watercress

Grate or crumble blue cheese. Put soft cheese into a bowl,

and beat to a soft cream with the milk and wine. Beat in the blue cheese and season to taste with salt and pepper.

Shape into a thick sausage shape (it's a bit sticky, but roll lightly with your fingertips, like Plasticine). Wrap in plastic film, put on a plate and leave in the fridge for at least half an hour.

Serve as pâté, with thin hot toast and butter or French bread, or for a more formal starter, cut the roll into slices and arrange several slices on each small plate and garnish with walnut halves and watercress. It is delicious served with fresh fruit – grapes, apples, pears, nectarines etc.

The pâté can be frozen after wrapping in plastic film. Allow about an hour for it to defrost before serving, and store in the fridge until needed.

PEAR AND CHEESE TOAST   *Serves 1*

A delicious snack or starter. Use whatever cheese pleases your taste – Cheddar, Edam, Lancashire, Caerphilly or Stilton are lovely.

Preparation and cooking time: 10 minutes.

1 ripe eating pear
1–2 oz/25–50g cheese
1–2 slices of bread – granary is delicious
Little butter for spreading

Peel and core pear, and cut into thin slices. Slice cheese thinly. Toast bread lightly on both sides and spread with butter. Arrange pear slices on the toast, and top with slices of cheese. Put back under the hot grill for a few minutes, until cheese is golden and melted.

Serve at once.

BAKED EGGS

Serves 1 or 2

Very quick and easy to make. Can be eaten as a lunch or supper, or served in individual ramekins as a tasty starter. Use cheese or mushrooms in the recipe, or both if you're feeling extravagant!

Preparation and cooking time: 20–25 minutes.

Heat oven – 180°C/350°F/gas 4–5. Grease an individual dish or 2 ramekins.

CHEESE EGGS

2–3 oz/50–75g Cheddar cheese
2 eggs
Salt, pepper
Large knob of butter

Grate cheese and put half into the dish or dishes. Break eggs one at a time into a cup, then carefully slide them on top of the cheese. Season well with salt and pepper and cover with rest of cheese. Dot with butter.

Put dish or dishes onto a baking tray, and bake in the hot oven for 10–15 minutes, until the eggs are just set and the cheese is bubbling.

Serve with hot, granary bread.

MUSHROOM EGGS

2 oz/50g mushrooms
2 eggs
2 tblsp double cream or plain yoghurt
Salt, pepper
Large knob of butter

Wash and slice mushrooms and put them into the dish or dishes. Break eggs one at a time into a cup, then carefully slide them on top of the mushrooms. Spoon cream or yoghurt over the eggs, season with salt and pepper and dot with butter.

Cook and serve as for Cheese Eggs.

FRENCH OMELETTE   1 omelette

Everyone's instant answer to a request for a vegetarian meal! It is the best known type of omelette: light golden egg, folded over into an envelope shape. Served plain or with a wide variety of sweet or savoury fillings, folded inside. There is no need for a special omelette pan (unless you happen to own one, of course). Use any clean ordinary frying pan.

Preparation and cooking time: 10 minutes.

2–3 eggs
1 tsp cold water per egg
Pinch of salt and pepper (omit for sweet omelette)
Knob of butter
Filling as required (see below)

Prepare filling (see pages 27–28). Warm a plate, Break eggs

into a small basin, add water, salt and pepper and beat well with a fork.

Put butter into a frying pan and heat over a moderate heat until it is sizzling (but not brown). Pour egg mixture over the hot butter. Carefully, with a wide bladed knife or wooden spatula, draw the mixture from the middle to the sides of the pan, so that the uncooked egg in the middle can run onto the hot pan and set. Continue until all the egg is very lightly cooked underneath and the top is still runny and soft (about one minute). The top will cook in its own heat when it is folded over.

With the wide-bladed knife or fish slice, loosen the omelette so that you can remove it easily from the pan. Put filling across the middle of the omelette and fold both sides over it to make an envelope. If using a cold filling, cook for a further minute to heat it through. Tip omelette onto the warm plate. Serve at once, with French bread, bread rolls, sauté or new potatoes, a side salad or just a sliced fresh tomato.

OMELETTE OR PANCAKE FILLINGS

Savoury

Fresh or diced herbs – Add 1 tsp chopped or scissor-snipped herbs to the beaten eggs.

Cheese – 1–2 oz/25–50g grated or finely cubed.

Mushrooms – Wash and chop 4–5/2 oz/50g mushrooms. Cook gently in a small pan with a knob of butter, for 2–3 minutes, stirring occasionally. Keep hot.

Tomato – Wash 1–2 tomatoes, slice and fry in a little hot oil and keep hot. Or slice and use raw.

Asparagus – ½ small can (10 oz/298g size) asparagus tips.

Heat through gently in a small saucepan. Keep hot.

Onion and Peppers – Peel and chop a small onion. Wash, de-seed and chop half a small pepper. Fry gently for 4–5 minutes in a little vegetable oil, until soft. Keep hot.

Mixed vegetables – Cook 3–4 tblsp frozen mixed vegetables according to instructions on the packet. Drain and keep hot.

Sweet

Jam – Add 1–2 tblsp jam or bramble jelly. Warm jar gently by standing it in a saucepan with 2"/5cm hot water over a low heat.

Fruit – Add 2–3 tblsp sliced, tinned fruit (peaches, apricots, pineapple etc.)
or
Use 2–3 tblsp fresh fruit (bananas, peaches, strawberries, raspberries etc).

Marmalade – Add 2–3 tblsp orange or ginger marmalade.

Honey – Add 2–3 tblsp honey. Warm, as jam, if liked.

Honey and Walnut – Use 2–3 tblsp honey and 2 tblsp chopped walnuts.

Chocolate – Sprinkle 2 tblsp drinking chocolate over omelette or pancakes. Dot with a few dabs of butter and fold over carefully.

Sprinkle sweet omelettes with 1 tsp icing or granulated sugar, just before serving.

SPANISH OMELETTE   *1 Omelette*

A delicious omelette with a savoury filling, easily adapted to suit the tastes of all members of the family by the use of different "extras". Served flat like a thick pancake, mixed with onion, potato and other vegetables it's a good way of using up cold, cooked left-overs. (A large omelette, made with 4 eggs and some extra vegetables can be cut in half, serving 2 people.)

Preparation and cooking time: 15 minutes.

1 small onion
2–3 boiled potatoes
2–3 eggs
1 tsp cold water per egg
Salt, pepper
Pinch of mixed herbs (optional)
1 tblsp vegetable oil for frying

Prepare any "extras" if used (see overleaf). Peel and chop onion. Dice cooked potatoes. (Peel raw potatoes, dice and cook in boiling water for 5 minutes until soft.)

Beat eggs, water, salt and pepper and herbs lightly with a fork in a small basin.

Heat oil in an omelette or small frying pan over a medium heat and fry onion for 3–5 minutes until soft. Add diced potato and continue frying until potato is thoroughly heated. Add any "extras" and heat through again. Heat the grill and warm a plate. Pour beaten egg mixture into the pan over the vegetables, and cook without stirring until the bottom is firm, but the top remains creamy and moist (about 1–2 minutes). Shake pan occasionally to prevent egg sticking.

Place pan under hot grill for a few seconds, until the top is set – beware in case pan handle gets hot. Slide the omelette flat onto the warm plate and serve at once.

"Extras"

Vegetables – 1–2 tblsp cold cooked vegetables (peas, sweetcorn, green beans, mixed vegetables)

Sweet Peppers – 1–2 tblsp red or green peppers, chopped and mixed with the onion before frying.

Mushrooms – 3–4 mushrooms, washed and thinly sliced.

PANCAKES   *6–8 pancakes*

These can be sweet or savoury and are delicious any day, not just on Shrove Tuesday (Pancake Day). There are so many fillings you can put in pancakes – cheese, herbs, mushroom, tomatoes, cooked vegetables, jam, honey, chocolate, fruit etc. – that you should be able to find something to please even the most fussy member of the family – see page 27.

Preparation time: 10 minutes (plus 1 minute per pancake cooking time).

4 oz/100g/4 heaped tblsp plain flour
Pinch of salt
1 egg
½ pt/284ml/2 cups milk
Oil for frying

Prepare filling. Put flour and salt into a bowl, add the egg and mix it into the flour. Gradually add the milk and beat to make a smooth batter – the easy way is to use an electric or hand mixer, but with a bit more effort you can use a wooden spoon or a fork.

    Heat a clean frying pan over a moderate heat and when

hot, but not burning, grease the pan with a little oil (about ½ tsp). Pour enough batter to cover the pan thinly, and fry briskly until just set on top and lightly browned underneath, shaking pan occasionally to stop pancake sticking. Toss pancake (or flip it over with a knife) and fry for a few more moments to brown the other side. Turn pancake onto a warm plate, add chosen filling (a squeeze of lemon and shake of sugar is the traditional English filling) and roll it up or fold it into four. Wipe the pan with a pad of kitchen paper, re-heat and re-grease the pan, then cook the next pancake as before.

Pancakes taste best eaten at once, straight from the pan (I encourage my family to cook their own, as you can find yourself standing at the stove for hours!), but they can be filled, rolled up and kept warm while you cook the rest, or stacked flat on a plate in a warm oven until you've cooked all the batter.

Pancakes can be frozen, either filled and ready to defrost and reheat in the oven, or flat, unfilled, when they can be quickly defrosted and used when needed.

PIZZA   *Makes 2 generous portions*

There are generally (except in Norway) so many shapes and sizes of pizzas, both fresh and frozen, suitable for vegetarians on sale in the shops now, that it hardly seems worth the effort of making your own. However, this frying pan pizza recipe is quick and delicious, and probably cheaper than bought ones.

Preparation and cooking time: 30 minutes.

Base:
4 oz/100g/4 very heaped tblsp self-raising flour (white or wholemeal)
Pinch of salt
2 tblsp vegetable oil
1–2 tblsp cold water
Little oil for frying

Topping:
1 small onion
1 clove of garlic or ¼ tsp ground garlic
1 tblsp vegetable oil
1 small (7 oz/230g) can of tomatoes or 3–4 fresh tomatoes – washed
1 tsp tomato purée or ketchup
½ tsp mixed herbs
Pinch of oregano
½ tsp granulated sugar
Dash of Worcester sauce
Salt, pepper
2–4 oz/50–100g grated or thinly sliced cheese (Mozzarella is traditional but more expensive, Cheddar or Edam are tasty and cheaper)

The Base: put flour and salt in bowl, make a "well" in centre of flour and measure in oil and 1 tblsp water. Mix to a soft dough, using a knife to work in the flour gradually, adding more water if mixture is too dry.

Knead lightly with floured hands to form a ball of dough, and roll this out to fit the base of a medium-size frying pan (8″/20cm) – you can use a floured rolling pin or you can press the dough flat with the palms of your hands.

The Topping: peel and chop onion and fresh garlic. Heat oil in saucepan over a medium heat, and fry onion and garlic for 5 minutes, until softened but not browned. Chop tomatoes, add to onions, with tomato purée or ketchup, herbs, sugar, Worcester sauce and salt and pepper. Stir well, and simmer for 3–5 minutes to make a thick but slightly runny sauce.

Heat 1 tblsp oil in a clean frying pan over a moderate heat, carefully ease pizza base into pan (*mind the hot oil!*) and fry for 3–4 minutes on each side, lowering heat if it gets too brown. Remove pan from heat, spread tomato mixture on top, almost to the edges, as it will spread a bit. Add any extras, top with grated or thinly sliced cheese, and put under a hot grill for 3–5 minutes until golden brown, bubbly and delicious.

A few "extras" – just a few suggestions (I'm sure you have plenty of your own ideas) to use with your home-made pizza. Spread them over the tomato topping, or improve bought pizzas by adding them during cooking, either when under the grill or in the oven according to the instructions on the packet. Spread the extras over the top of the pizza and grill for 5–10 minutes.

Cheese – this is best on the very top of all the extras. Use
  Mozzarella, Cheddar or Edam, grated or thinly sliced.
Mushroom – wash and thinly slice, scatter over pizza.
Olives – stone and arrange on top of pizza.
Onion – slice very thinly, spread over topping.
Peppers – green or red, slice thinly and decorate with
  pepper rings or chop thinly and scatter over pizza.
Sweetcorn – sprinkle 1–2 tblsp over pizza.
Tomato – slice thinly, arrange on top of pizza.
Pineapple – chop and scatter over topping.

If using several extras, cook each layer before adding the

next layer, putting the cheese on the very top to give a melting, crispy topping.

You can make an "Instant" French bread pizza using the "topping" recipe as given on page 33, and spreading this over a length of split French loaf, adding any extras and browning under a hot grill for 2–3 minutes, until the cheese is melting and golden.

EGG MAYONNAISE

1 main meal or a starter for 2 people.

A light summer lunch or supper, or a nice starter if you are entertaining in style. It's accepted as "normal" food by non-vegetarians!

Preparation and cooking time: 20 minutes.

2 eggs
Few lettuce leaves
Small chunk of cucumber
1–2 tomatoes
Few rings of green or red pepper
2–3 tblsp mayonnaise – preferably home-made, see page 181
Dash of paprika pepper

Hard boil the eggs – simmer for 10 minutes in salted water. Cool in cold water, peel and rinse eggs to get rid of all the shell.

Wash and dry lettuce, shred finely. Wash and slice cucumber, tomato and pepper.

Arrange a bed of lettuce on 1 or 2 plates.

Slice eggs in rings, or cut in half lengthways and arrange on the lettuce (with the cut side facing down if halved). Arrange cucumber, tomato and peppers at side of eggs.

Coat top of eggs with the chosen mayonnaise and garnish with paprika pepper.

CHEESE FONDUE   *Serves 2*

You can use a proper fondue pot with burners if you have one, or a small, thick saucepan. Cheese fondue will work quite well without a burner (it does not need to be boiling like an oil fondue) or you can use a hotplate to keep it warm if you have one. The fondue can be gently reheated on the stove if you're very slow in eating it. Forks can be used instead of fondue sticks.

Preparation and cooking time: 20 minutes.

1 small French stick
1 clove of fresh garlic

4 oz/100g Gruyère
4 oz/100g Emmenthal

} You can substitute with Cheddar on its own, or mix it with Edam or other hard cheeses; this is cheaper than Gruyère or Emmenthal

2 tsp cornflour or flour
¼ pt/142ml/1 cup dry white wine or cider
1 tsp lemon juice
1 tsp herb or whole grain mustard (optional but gives a good taste)
Shake of black pepper

Cut French bread into bite-sized chunks and place in a

serving bowl.

Peel garlic clove, cut it in half and crush it around base and sides of fondue pot. Discard garlic pieces.

Grate chosen cheeses.

Put cornflour or flour into a cup or small basin and mix to a smooth paste with 2 tblsp of the wine or cider.

Pour remaining wine or cider into fondue pot, add lemon juice and heat gently over a low heat, gradually stirring in grated cheese and mustard (if used), with a wooden spoon (a metal one will get too hot to hold). Continue stirring until cheese has melted. Remove from heat.

Stir cornflour mixture again, then mix it into the fondue mixture. Return pot to the heat and stir fondue well until the mixture is thick, smooth and just bubbling. Season with black pepper.

Carefully carry hot fondue pot to the table and place on the burner (if you have one) over a low flame, or put on a hot plate or thick table mat.

Always use the correct fuel recommended for your fondue set (generally methylated spirit) and put the burner in place on the table before lighting it, never carry a lighted burner from kitchen to table!!

If you don't want to use alcohol in your fondue, apple juice or non-alcoholic wine will be a good substitute.

WARM LETTUCE AND PEANUT SALAD
Serves 1–2

Different from the usual salad mixture. I like to use the "fancy" lettuces for this salad – endive, radiccio, webb, cos or even Chinese leaves. Supermarkets sell prepared mixtures of these lettuces, which is an economical way of buying several different types of lettuce in small amounts, and these are excellent for this recipe.

Preparation and cooking time: 10 minutes.

Portion of lettuce – a mixture of colours and textures looks
    most attractive
1 thick slice of bread – wholemeal or white
2 tblsp oil – both olive and walnut oil have a lovely flavour, but
    any vegetable oil is acceptable
2 tsp wine vinegar
2 tblsp/2 oz/50g salted peanuts

Wash and thoroughly dry lettuce, shred coarsely and put into salad bowl. Cut bread into ½"/1cm cubes. Heat oil in a frying pan over a moderate heat and fry bread cubes for a few minutes turning frequently, until evenly browned and crispy.

Dress lettuce by tossing it in the wine vinegar, then pour over the fried bread cubes and any oil left in the pan. Add peanuts and turn the mixture well in the bowl.

Serve at once, while still warm.

SAVOURY FRUIT SALAD   *Serves 2–4*

An intriguing taste of sweet and savoury, which can be enjoyed by all the family as an accompaniment to hot or cold dishes.

Preparation and cooking time: 15 minutes.

½ small onion or 2–3 spring onions
2 sticks of celery
Small bunch of seedless grapes
2 oz/50g/2 tblsp walnut halves
1 green eating apple
1 red eating apple
1 eating pear
1 tblsp lemon juice
1–2 tblsp vinaigrette dressing – see page 182

Peel onion and cut into thin rings, or wash, trim and slice spring onions. Wash and trim celery, and cut into ½"/1cm lengths. Wash seedless grapes and drain well. Roughly chop walnuts. Wash apples, cut into quarters and remove cores, slice thinly and place in a bowl. Peel, core and thinly slice pear, and mix with the apples. Stir in lemon juice and mix thoroughly to coat the fruit to stop it browning.

Add onion, celery, grapes and walnuts to the fruit. Pour over the vinaigrette dressing and toss lightly.

Cover with plastic film and chill in the fridge until needed.

CREOLE SALAD   *Serves 2–3*

This salad can be enjoyed by non-vegetarians, and used as an accompaniment to various dishes; we like it particularly with vegetable gougère. It's a good way to use up left-overs, cooked rice, etc. If you want to make a smaller amount, just use less rice and cut down on the amount of fruit, nuts and dressing.

Try to make it at least one hour before eating, so that the salad can absorb the flavour from the mayonnaise.

Preparation and cooking time: 30 minutes (or 15 minutes if rice is already cooked).

1 cup uncooked brown or patna (long grain type) rice
or 2 cups cooked rice
1–2 bananas
1 eating apple – red or green, leave the skin on
1–2 tblsp lemon juice (juice of ½ lemon)
Tiny bunch of seedless grapes
1–2 slices of pineapple
2 tblsp sultanas
½ cup chopped walnuts or pecan nuts
1 tblsp grated coconut (optional)

Dressing
3–4 tblsp mayonnaise (see page 181)
1 tblsp lemon juice (use rest of the lemon)
Pinch chilli powder or cayenne pepper
½ tsp mustard

Cook rice (see page 48), drain, rinse and leave to cool.
   Peel and slice bananas, wash, core and slice apple (do not peel) and turn these slices of fruit in the lemon juice to stop them going brown.
   Wash grapes, cut pineapple into small pieces.
   Wash sultanas and drain.
   Mix fruit and nuts with the cooked rice.

The Dressing
Mix mayonnaise with all the other dressing ingredients, seasoning to taste with the chilli powder or cayenne pepper.
   Stir mayonnaise mixture thoroughly into rice mixture.
   Tip into serving dish, sprinkle with coconut if liked.
   Cover dish and leave in fridge until needed.
   This salad looks attractive served on a flat dish or on a bed of washed lettuce or watercress, but it is supposed to be a

white salad, so do not sprinkle with parsley.

LIZA'S POTATO SALAD   *Plenty for 2-3*

Named after our blonde Danish friend who always serves
this salad with super barbeques by the swimming pool.

*Preparation and cooking time: 30 minutes (the potatoes can be
cooked in advance and kept in the fridge until needed).*

½ lb/225g new potatoes (these are really delicious)
or 3–4 old potatoes (the waxy type)
Salt
Sprig of mint
1 egg
2 tblsp mayonnaise (bought or home-made, see page 181)
Few sprigs of parsley and/or chives

Scrub new potatoes or peel old ones and cut them into large,
bite-sized chunks. Cook potatoes in boiling salted water
with a sprig of mint for 5–10 minutes, being careful not to let
the potatoes get too soft or crumble.

Hard boil the egg (simmer in boiling salted water for 10
minutes). Plunge egg into cold water, peel off the shell and
cut into 8–10 pieces.

Remove potatoes from heat when cooked, drain at once
and rinse in cold water to stop them cooking any more.
Remove mint, and leave the potatoes to drain and cool
completely.

Cut new potatoes into chunks if too big, and mix potato

pieces with the mayonnaise. When all the pieces are coated, carefully mix in the pieces of egg, trying not to break them up.

Pile into a serving dish, and sprinkle with washed, scissor-snipped parsley and/or chives.

COLESLAW
1–2 helpings

A cheap tasty salad or accompaniment to hot dishes or barbeques. A good way of using up small amounts of left-over new vegetables, and much tastier than the bought sort.

Preparation time: 15 minutes.

1 "slice" of crisp hard cabbage, white or green
1 small carrot
1 small onion
1 eating apple (red skinned if available)
1 tsp lemon juice
1–2 tblsp mayonnaise (see page 181)
Salt, pepper

Trim outer leaves and stalk of cabbage. Shred it finely, wash in cold water and drain well. Scrape carrot and chop, shred or coarsely grate it. Peel and chop or finely slice onion. Wash and core apple, shred, finely slice or chop it and mix with lemon juice to prevent it browning.

Mix all the fruit and vegetables together in a bowl, stirring in the mayonnaise and turning it gently until all the ingredients are well coated. Season to taste with salt and pepper.

Variations

Many different fruits or vegetables can be added to the basic recipe. Try a tblsp of chopped, salted nuts, a handful of washed, drained sultanas, a washed chopped green or red pepper, 1 or 2 stalks of washed and chopped celery, or a few slices of cucumber for a change.

TABBOULEH   *Serves 1–2 according to appetite*

This salad makes a more unusual accompaniment at buffet meals or barbeques. It can be enjoyed by all the family, not just the vegetarian members. Tabbouleh will keep for a few days in a covered bowl in the fridge.

Preparation time: 10 minutes (plus 1 hour for soaking).

4 oz/100g/4 very heaped tblsp bulgar or cracked wheat
3–4 spring onions
Small bunch of chives
Small bunch of parsley } **Use a mixture of herbs; it**
Small bunch of mint **should be as green as possible**
2–3 tblsp olive oil or vegetable oil
2 tblsp lemon juice (juice of ½ lemon)
Salt, pepper

Put bulgar or cracked wheat in a bowl, half fill bowl with cold water and leave wheat to soak for an hour.

Strain well in a sieve, and squeeze as dry as possible.

Dry the bowl and tip wheat back into it.

Trim and wash spring onions (cut off roots and any yellow leaves, leaving as much of the green as looks appetising). Chop or scissor-snip the onions into the wheat.

Wash and scissor-snip chives and parsley into the wheat.

Strip leaves off mint stalks, rinse leaves in cold water and chop or scissor-snip them finely into wheat mixture.

Mix wheat and herbs well together, add oil and season to taste with lemon juice, salt and pepper.

If you have fresh herbs in the garden, experiment by adding a few washed, scissor-snipped sprigs of thyme, rosemary, lemon, tarragon, etc. with the other herbs, according to taste and availability.

MIXED BEAN SALAD   *Serves 2*

Make at least enough for 2 people, so that you can use a good mixture of ingredients. This is a good recipe for using up the odds and ends of left-over or extra cooked or canned beans. It's hardly worth cooking dried beans specially as you need such a small amount of each kind (unless, of course, you are making a huge salad for a party dish).

Preparation time: 10 minutes.

2 tblsp cooked or canned kidney beans (see page 74)
2 tblsp cooked or canned white beans i.e. Barlotti, Cannellini
       or haricot
1 tblsp chick peas, cooked or canned
2 tblsp cooked or canned sweetcorn (the canned sweetcorn with
       pepper is rather nice)
½ small onion or 1–2 spring onions
1 stick of celery
1 tblsp vinaigrette dressing (see page 182), or slimmer's salad
       dressing (see page 184) or yoghurt dressing (see page 184)
Salt, pepper
Few sprigs of parsley or chives

Rinse canned beans and chick peas in cold water, drain cooked or canned beans and put all the beans, peas and sweetcorn into a basin.

Peel and finely chop onion or trim, wash and slice spring onion. Wash and chop celery, and add onion and celery to the bean mixture.

Stir in chosen salad dressing, mix well and spoon into a serving dish or individual side dishes. Sprinkle with washed, snipped parsley and chives.

GREEK SALAD   *1 individual salad*

Usually served as a side dish, but the cheese makes it filling enough to have a nice large helping as a light lunch on a hot day.

Preparation time: 10 minutes.

½ small onion
1 tblsp vinaigrette dressing (preferably made with olive oil for
          the best flavour) see page 182
2″/5cm chunk of cucumber
1–2 tomatoes
Few black olives
2 oz/50g Greek Feta cheese – if you can't get Feta, use a
          crumbly white cheese; Lancashire is good

Peel and slice onion, and put into a basin with the vinaigrette dressing. Peel cucumber, cut into dice, wash and slice tomatoes and add both to onion mixture with the olives, stirring well to mix with the dressing. Dice cheese. Pour salad into serving dish, sprinkle cheese dice over the top. Serve as a side salad or with warm pitta bread or bread rolls as a light lunch.

AVOCADO SALAD   *Fills one avocado half*

This must be my daughter's favourite lunch; she has it so often. It also makes a good dinner party starter, using small avocados. You can use any variety of salad vegetables available, but it's quite economical as you only need a very little of each to make a good filling.

Preparation time: 10 minutes.

Use a mixture of your favourite salad ingredients:
1 tomato
Small piece of green pepper
Small piece of red pepper
Small stalk of celery
2–3 rings of onion
1–2 spring onions
Small piece of carrot
Handful of fresh chives
½ large avocado pear
1 oz/25g Cheddar, Edam, Double Gloucester, etc. cheese
1–2 tsp lemon juice, vinaigrette or slimmer's salad dressing
**   (see pages 182, 184)**

Prepare salad vegetables according to type – wash and chop tomato, peppers and celery, peel and very finely chop onion, trim and slice spring onion, peel and coarsely grate or finely chop carrot. Wash and scissor-snip chives, and mix all the vegetables together in a basin. Halve avocado, remove stone and scoop out some of the avocado flesh with a teaspoon, but leave enough flesh on the skin to ensure a firm shell. Chop scooped-out avocado into cubes and add to vegetables. Coarsely grate or cube the chosen cheese and add to the vegetable mixture. Mix in lemon juice or salad dressing, and spoon the filling into avocado shells. Looks nice served in a glass avocado dish or a small wooden bowl garnished with lettuce or Chinese leaves.

If you are making this in advance, brush avocado shell with lemon juice, and toss diced avocado in lemon juice to stop it browning. Cover filled avocado with plastic film and leave in the fridge until needed.

CRUDITÉS   *Serves 1*

A firm favourite here since someone in our house worked in a bistro during her year out and served this dish frequently. Nice as a starter or light snack. Use a good variety of raw vegetables cut into finger-sized sticks or bite-sized chunks, and serve the dip in little individual pots or dishes.

Preparation time: 10–15 minutes plus time for making home-made mayonnaise if used.

For each serving prepare a small stack of several different raw vegetables, and one or two pots of dips.

Vegetables
1 carrot
1 length of cucumber – 2″/5cm
1–2 sticks of celery
½ small red or green pepper, cut lengthways
Few cauliflower florets
Few radishes

3 or 4 mushrooms
Few tiny spring onions

Dips
2–3 tblsp mayonnaise, home-made (page 181) or bought, either
plain or flavoured with garlic, curry powder, tomato
purée or blue cheese
Crisp lettuce or watercress for garnish.

Prepare vegetables – peel carrot and cut into sticks; wash
cucumber and cut lengthways into sticks; trim and wash
celery and cut into thin lengths; wash pepper and remove
seeds, cut in half lengthways and slice into fingers; wash cauliflower, break carefully into small florets; wash and slice
mushrooms if large; trim and wash spring onions.

Mix chosen mayonnaise (if you don't have home-made
you can buy "fresh mayonnaise" in the supermarket or use a
good quality bottled one) with different chosen flavourings:

Garlic – beat in ¼ tsp garlic paste or powder
Curry – beat in ¼ tsp curry powder, cayenne pepper or few
    drops hot pepper sauce.
Rosé – beat in ½ tsp tomato purée or ketchup
Blue cheese – beat 1 oz/25g blue cheese to a paste, and mix
    it into the mayonnaise.

Spoon dips into individual pots. Serve crudités on a plate,
with the pot of dip surrounded by little piles of vegetables,
garnished with washed crisp lettuce or watercress.

Hummus, Tsatsiki, cheese, avocado or watercress dip can
all be served in the same way. For a party, serve large dishes
of dips, with crudités, crisps or pieces of pitta bread.

RICE, PASTA, POTATOES AND PASTRY

Cooked pasta can be served in numerous ways, on its own instead of potatoes, just tossed in a little butter, cream or yoghurt and sprinkled with fresh snipped herbs, or made into a meal mixed with home-made sauce or topped with sauce and/or cheese and baked in the oven.

Rice can also be served instead of potatoes, or mixed with vegetables and nuts to make a meal in itself.

Some of the dishes in this section can be eaten hot or cold and are suitable for a packed lunch or picnic.

BOILED RICE

Allow ½ cup/2 oz/50g dry rice per person for an average serving.

Rice is a good standby to serve with all kinds of dishes, and it saves time peeling potatoes. Use long grain or Patna type rice for savoury dishes; the smaller round grain rice is used for puddings. Brown rice is whole unrefined rice (the equivalent of wholemeal bread), and so has all the nutrients left in it. Use either brown or white Patna type rice as you prefer, but remember the brown rice takes a little longer to cook than the more refined white rice. You can also buy prepared and "easy cook" rice of several types in most supermarkets, which should be cooked exactly as described on the packet. This type of rice is very good and easy to cook, but is usually more expensive than plain, long grain brown or white rice. There are many ways of cooking rice; two of the easiest ways are described below:-

METHOD ONE

I prefer to use this method, as I tend to let the pan boil dry with the second method. However, you do need a fairly large pan (especially if cooking for the whole family) and it's a bit steamy as the rice must be cooked without the lid on, otherwise it all boils over.

Preparation and cooking time: 30–35 minutes for brown rice
12–15 minutes for white rice.

For each serving allow:
½ cup/2oz/50g long grain rice
Pinch of salt
Few sprigs of fresh parsley or chives

Wash the rice well to get rid of the starch (put it into a saucepan and slosh it around in several rinses of cold water). Put rice into a large saucepan, and fill pan two-thirds full of boiling water. Add ½–1 tsp salt (according to amount of rice), bring back to the boil and boil gently, with the lid off the pan, for:

25–30 minutes for brown rice
10–12 minutes for white rice

until rice is just cooked but still firm. Do not over-cook or it will go sticky and puddingy. Drain well, fluff with a fork, and serve garnished with washed, scissor-snipped parsley or chives.

METHOD TWO
Be careful that the rice doesn't boil dry.

Preparation and cooking time: 35–40 minutes for brown rice
                             13–16 minutes for white rice.

For each serving allow:
½ cup/2 oz/50g long grain rice
1 tsp vegetable oil or small knob of butter
1½ cups/8 fl oz/215ml boiling water if using brown rice
or
1 cup/¼ pt/142ml boiling water if using white rice
Pinch of salt
Few sprigs of fresh parsley or chives.

Wash the rice as in method one. Put vegetable oil or butter in a small saucepan and heat gently. Then add the rice, stirring all the time, to coat each grain. Add the required amount of boiling water and a pinch of salt, bring to simmering point and stir. Put on the lid, and leave rice to simmer over a gentle heat for:

30–35 minutes for brown rice
12–15 minutes for white rice.

Test to see if the rice is cooked: all the liquid should be absorbed and the rice should be cooked but not soggy. Lightly fluff with a fork, and serve garnished with washed scissor-snipped parsley or chives.

FRIED RICE

You can either use up left-over boiled rice (I always cook too much) or cook some specially.

Preparation and cooking time: 15 minutes (15-40 minutes if you have to boil the rice first, according to type of rice).

For each serving allow:
1 cup boiled rice (use ½ cup dry rice)
½ onion or 1–2 spring onions
1 tblsp vegetable oil
Few sprigs of fresh herbs – parsley, chives, mint, tarragon etc.

Optional extras:
1–2 mushrooms, sliced
1 tblsp frozen peas
1 tblsp pine kernels
1–2 tblsp cashew nuts
1 tblsp canned sweetcorn

Cook rice if necessary (see page 49). Peel and chop onion or trim, wash and chop spring onions. Heat oil in a frying pan over a medium heat, add chopped onion and fry, turning frequently for 2–3 minutes, until soft. Add cooked rice and fry for a further 4–5 minutes, stirring all the time. Add any extras if used (the peas can be cooked from frozen, they will defrost in the pan) and cook for a further 2–3 minutes, stirring all the time until it is all heated through. Garnish with the washed, scissor-snipped herbs.

You can make this more substantial by adding larger amounts of vegetables and sprinkling with a little grated cheese.

RISOTTO   *Serves 1*

A tasty, cheap and cheerful meal, quickly assembled from larder or fridge. It's easy to make a larger quantity, reserve one portion for the vegetarian and add cold, cooked meat instead of nuts to suit the non-vegetarian members of the family.

Preparation and cooking time: 30 minutes.

2 oz/50g/½ cup long grain rice (uncooked) – white or brown
1 small onion
1 clove of garlic or ¼ tsp powdered garlic
1 stick of celery
2–3 mushrooms
1 tomato
Few rings of green or red pepper
1 tblsp vegetable oil for frying
½ vegetable stock cube
1 cup/¼ pt/142ml boiling water
1 tblsp cooked peas
1 tblsp cooked or canned sweetcorn
1 hard-boiled egg
2 tblsp pine nut kernels or cashew nuts or broken walnuts

Salt, pepper
Worcester sauce
1 oz/25g Cheddar or Edam cheese – grated
1 tsp Parmesan cheese

Wash rice in several rinses of cold water to get rid of the
starch.

Peel and chop onion and garlic. Wash and chop celery.
Wash and slice mushrooms and tomato and chop pepper.

Heat oil in a saucepan over a moderate heat and fry onion,
garlic and celery for 4–5 minutes until softened but not
brown. Add washed, drained rice and continue to fry,
stirring well for a further 3 minutes. Stir in chopped pepper.
Dissolve stock cube in the boiling water and add stock to rice
mixture. Stir well and leave to simmer with lid on, stirring
occasionally for 10–12 minutes until rice is tender and stock
is almost absorbed – add a little more liquid if rice is not
cooked (brown rice may need this).

Add mushrooms, tomato, peas, sweetcorn, sliced hard-
boiled egg and pine kernels or cashew nuts and continue to
cook for a further 3–5 minutes stirring gently, until heated
right through. Season with salt, pepper and Worcester sauce.

Serve with lots of grated cheese and a sprinkle of
Parmesan.

PASTA

Allow 1 very full cup/3 oz/75g dry pasta – shells, bows,
spaghetti, etc. per person.
Allow 3–4 sheets dry lasagne per serving.

There are numerous shapes of pasta, but they are all cooked
in the same way, and most of the different shapes are

interchangeable in most recipes, with the exception of the lasagne and cannelloni types. Many types of pasta are now available in white or wholemeal form, so choose which you prefer, but remember to allow a little extra cooking time for wholemeal pasta. I think wholemeal pasta is more filling than white pasta, but that may just be my imagination! Green pasta, flavoured with spinach, is also available. It looks most attractive.

Spaghetti – available in various lengths and thickness.
Tagliatelle and other noodle varieties – sold in strands and bunches.
Fancy shapes – shells, bows, spirals etc.
Macaroni – thick tubular shapes.
Lasagne – large flat sheets.
Cannelloni – rolled pasta sheets filled with a tasty stuffing.
Ravioli – little pasta envelopes filled with a savoury stuffing.

Fresh pasta is now becoming widely available, sold from super pasta "boutiques", and is made in lots of shapes and sizes. It can be bought with a wide choice of sauces and stuffings, using tomatoes, ricotta cheese, nuts, spinach and lots of herbs and spices. Fresh pasta cooks very quickly, needing only a minute or two in boiling, salted water with a little oil, or cooking in the sauce in a moderate oven (enquire about exact cooking instructions when you buy the pasta).

Most makes of dry pasta have the cooking instructions on the packet, and the best advice is to follow these carefully.

Allow approximately 1 cup/3 oz/75g per serving. Dry and fresh pasta must be cooked in a large pan of boiling, salted water, with a tsp of vegetable oil added to the water to help stop the pasta sticking. Long spaghetti is stood in the pan and pushed down gradually as it softens. Let the water come to the boil, then lower heat and leave to simmer (without the lid or it will boil over) for

10–12 minutes – dry wholemeal pasta
 8–10 minutes – dry white pasta
 2–4   minutes – fresh pasta

until pasta is just cooked (*al dente*). Drain well, in a colander preferably, otherwise you run the risk of losing the pasta down the sink. Serve at once topped with a little butter, or yoghurt and a sprinkle of parsley or with a sauce.

PASTA AND AUBERGINE BAKE   *Serves 2*

An intriguing compromise between lasagne and moussaka using pasta shapes. It's better to make enough for two; the second portion can be frozen ready for defrosting and baking later.

Preparation and cooking time: 45–50 minutes plus draining time for aubergines.

1 medium-size aubergine
Salt, pepper
6 oz/150g/2 full cups dry pasta shapes – shells, bows, etc. Use wholemeal pasta if possible.
2–3 tblsp vegetable oil
1 onion
1 clove of fresh garlic or ¼ tsp garlic powder
2 tomatoes – fresh or canned
1 tblsp tomato purée or ketchup   *(continued overleaf)*

(Pasta and Aubergine Bake continued)

½ tsp mixed herbs
¼ tsp cayenne pepper (optional)
Few drops of pepper sauce (optional)
¼ tsp sugar
2–3 tblsp juice from canned tomatoes or water
2 oz/50g Cheddar or Edam cheese, grated
1 tblsp grated Parmesan cheese

Heat oven – 190°C/375°F/gas 5–6. Grease an oven-proof dish or 2 individual dishes. Trim, wash and slice aubergine and put into a colander, sprinkle with salt, stand colander on a plate and leave for about an hour to drain out the bitter juices.

Cook pasta shapes in boiling, salted water with ½ tsp vegetable oil until just tender (*al dente*), about 10 minutes or as instructed on the packet. Drain pasta.

Peel and chop onion and fresh garlic. Wash and chop fresh tomatoes. Heat 2 tblsp oil in a frying pan and fry onion, garlic and aubergine slices until softened and lightly golden, turning slices to colour both sides, adding a little more oil if needed. Stir in chopped tomatoes, tomato purée or ketchup, herbs, cayenne pepper and pepper sauce (if used), sugar, salt and pepper. Add 2 tblsp juice from canned tomatoes or cold water, and simmer gently for 5–10 minutes until vegetables are soft and sauce is nice and thick. Add a little more liquid if necessary.

Put a layer of vegetable mixture into the dishes, then a layer of pasta and then continue to alternate the layers until they are all used up, finishing with a vegetable layer. Sprinkle with grated Cheddar or Edam, and top with Parmesan. Bake for 20 minutes in the hot oven, until the cheese is melted and golden.

CREAMY NUT PASTA

Serves 1

A really quick, cheap and cheerful filling snack or supper, just add a bread roll and green salad if you're very hungry. You can use any pasta for this dish; spaghetti, shells, noodles, etc., but I think tagliatelli is the nicest. A small helping makes a good starter to a meal.

Preparation and cooking time: 20 minutes.

Salt, pepper
1 tsp cooking oil
3 oz/75g/1 full cup chosen pasta
1–2 tblsp cream cheese or curd cheese
1–2 tblsp yoghurt or soured cream or double cream
2 tblsp roughly chopped walnuts or cashew nuts*
Pinch of paprika pepper

Half fill a large saucepan with hot salted water, add oil and bring to the boil. Throw in pasta, stir and boil gently for 5–8 minutes until pasta is cooked *al dente* but not soggy. Drain pasta in colander or sieve.

   Put cream or curd cheese, yoghurt or cream and nuts into pasta saucepan, and stir over a very low heat until just beginning to melt. Add pasta to cream mixture and stir over a low heat until coated with cheese mixture. Season to taste and serve on a warm plate, topped with a shake of paprika.

* Chopped pecan nuts, hazel nuts or pine kernels can be used instead of walnuts or cashew nuts, according to what is in the larder.

LENTIL BOLOGNESE SAUCE   *2–3 helpings*

You can make half the quantity of this recipe, but it is just as easy to make enough for 2 helpings: use half with pasta today and keep the rest in the fridge to serve poured over a big jacket potato tomorrow, or freeze one portion in a covered foil dish for future use.

Preparation and cooking time: 30 minutes
                    plus 45 minutes (dried green lentils)
                    or plus 20 minutes (dried red lentils)

4 oz/100g/just over ½ cup dried green or red lentils
or 1 x 14 oz/397g can lentils
1 onion
1 clove of garlic or ¼ tsp ground garlic
2 sticks of celery
1 small carrot
1 small can (7 oz/230g) tomatoes or 3–4 fresh tomatoes
1 tblsp oil for frying
1 tblsp tomato purée or tomato ketchup
Salt, pepper
½ tsp sugar
1 tsp dried mixed herbs
½ tsp vegetable extract
1–2 cups/¼–½ pt/142–284ml water (save lentil water if cooking dried lentils or save liquid from can of lentils)

Wash the dried lentils well – no need to soak – then cook in boiling water (no salt) for 45 minutes if you are using green lentils or 20 minutes for red lentils. Drain lentils and save water to use in the sauce.

  Peel and chop onion and fresh garlic if used. Wash and

chop celery finely. Peel and grate or finely chop carrot. Chop tomatoes (use juice as well).

Heat oil in saucepan over a moderate heat and fry onion, celery and garlic gently for 5 minutes until softened.

Add carrot, cooked or canned lentils, tomatoes, tomato purée or ketchup, salt, pepper, sugar, herbs and vegetable extract. Then stir in 1–2 cups of water (you will need most water if using fresh tomatoes) to make a runny sauce. Bring to the boil over a low heat, stirring occasionally. Then simmer for 10–15 minutes, adding a little more liquid if it seems too stiff, until you have a nice thick sauce.

Note: If using the sauce for lasagne (page 61), with "no cook" lasagne strips, add a little more liquid to make a runny sauce, as the lasagne absorbs the extra liquid while cooking.

LEEK AND MUSHROOM BOLOGNESE SAUCE

2 helpings

A tasty, "different" Bolognese sauce, makes a nice lasagne filling. Use one portion, and freeze the second for another day.

Preparation and cooking time: 20–25 minutes.

2 medium-size leeks – you could use onions if leeks are unavailable
4 oz/100g mushrooms
1 small (7 oz/230g) can tomatoes
or 3–4 fresh tomatoes with ½ cup/2½ fl oz/70ml water
1 tblsp vegetable oil for frying
½ tsp mixed herbs   *(continued overleaf)*

(Leek and Mushroom Bolognese Sauce continued)

Salt, pepper
$\frac{1}{4}$ tsp sugar
Dash of Worcester and/or soy sauce

Clean leeks thoroughly: cut off roots and tough green leaves, just leaving any green that looks appetising; slit down one side and rinse the layers very well in cold running water to get rid of any soil and grit. It's a bit fiddly and takes a few minutes to get really clean.

Chop cleaned leeks into rings ($\frac{1}{4}$"/$\frac{1}{2}$cm) or peel and chop onions. Wash and slice mushrooms. Wash and chop fresh tomatoes, if used.

Heat oil in a saucepan over a moderate heat, fry leeks or onions for 4–5 minutes until soft. Add mushrooms, tinned tomatoes and juice or chopped fresh tomatoes and water, herbs, salt, pepper, sugar and sauces. Stir well, and simmer for 5–10 minutes to make a "saucy" consistency.

Note: If using the sauce for lasagne (page 61), with "no cook" lasagne strips, add a little more liquid to make a runny sauce, as the lasagne absorbs the extra liquid while cooking.

SPAGHETTI BOLOGNESE   *Serves 1 or 2*

Use the Bolognese sauce of your choice and serve sprinkled with plenty of grated cheese.

Preparation and cooking time: 15 minutes (plus time making the sauce).

1 or 2 portions:
Lentil Bolognese sauce – see page 58

or
Leek and Mushroom Bolognese sauce – see page 59
or
TSP Bolognese sauce – see page 164

Per Serving
3 oz/75g dry spaghetti
or 1 full cup/3 oz/75g pasta shells, bows, etc.
½ tsp salt
1 tsp vegetable oil
1 oz/25g grated Cheddar cheese
Little grated Parmesan cheese, if liked

Prepare (or defrost pre-cooked) Bolognese sauce. Cook spaghetti or chosen pasta in a large saucepan of boiling water, with ½ tsp salt and 1 tsp vegetable oil, for 10–12 minutes – make sure the water is boiling before putting the spaghetti in, and leave the lid off the pan or it will boil over. If using long spaghetti, stand the bundle of spaghetti in the boiling water, and as it softens coil it down into the water, without breaking the strands.

Drain pasta when just *al dente* and tip onto 1 or 2 warm plates. Pour hot sauce into centre of pasta and serve sprinkled with grated Cheddar and Parmesan cheese.

LASAGNE   *Serves 1 or 2*

Choose your favourite "flavour" of Bolognese sauce. "No-cook" type lasagne strips are the easiest to use, but remember to make the Bolognese sauce rather runny, to allow the pasta to absorb the extra liquid while baking.

Preparation and cooking time: 1 hour plus time for making Bolognese sauce.

Filling – For each person allow 1 serving of sauce
Lentil Bolognese sauce – see page 58
or
Leek and Mushroom Bolognese sauce – see page 59
or
TSP Bolognese sauce – see page 164

Cheese Sauce – For each person allow:
2 tsp flour or cornflour
¼ pt/142ml/1 cup milk
½ oz/15g butter or marg
2 oz/50g Cheddar or Edam cheese, grated
Salt, pepper, pinch of mustard

Pasta – For each person allow **3–4 strips lasagne** (preferably "no cook" type). If you can't get "no cook" lasagne, cook 3–4 strips lasagne for each person in a pan of salted water with 1 tsp oil, for 8–10 minutes or as directed on packet. Drain and use in layers as below. Do not add extra liquid to the chosen Bolognese sauce: it can be used fairly thick as the pasta will not need to absorb the extra liquid during baking.

Prepare chosen Bolognese sauce.

Heat oven – 180°C/350°F/gas 4–5.

Cheese Sauce – Mix flour or cornflour with a little of the milk in a small bowl or mug to make a runny paste. Boil rest of milk in pan, pour flour mixture over it, stir well over the heat, until it thickens. Beat in marg or butter, cheese and seasoning.

Use a deep, oven-proof dish, large enough for 2 if making double the quantity, or use an individual foil dish for each person. Pour half the Bolognese sauce into the dish, then add half the lasagne strips and half the cheese sauce. Continue to alternate the layers, ending with a cheese layer on top.

Bake in the hot oven for 35–40 minutes – large dish
or 25–30 minutes – individual dish.

POTATOES

BOILED POTATOES

When cooking boiled potatoes, choose potatoes of the same size to cook together, or cut large potatoes into evenly-sized pieces, so that all the potatoes will be cooked at the same time (very big potatoes will go soggy on the outside before the inside is cooked if left whole). Do not let the water boil too fast, or the potatoes will tend to break up.

Allow 2–4 potato pieces per serving.

Peel potatoes thinly, digging out any eyes or black bits with as little waste as possible. Put potatoes into a saucepan, cover with hot, salted water and bring to the boil, then lower the heat and simmer for 15–20 minutes until they feel just soft when tested with a knife. Drain and serve, or mash for a topping.

MASHED POTATOES – a good way of disguising boiled potatoes that have broken up during cooking! Prepare the boiled potatoes as described above, but the raw potatoes can be cut into thick slices and cooked for less time (approximately 10 minutes) until soft. Drain potatoes well, and mash with a fork or masher until fluffy. Use as a pie topping, plain or with extras (see below) or heap onto a serving dish and serve.

EXTRAS

Creamed – after mashing until fluffy, add a large knob of butter and a little top-of-the-milk. Beat well, flavouring with a dash of grated nutmeg if liked. Use as a topping or fork into a heap on a serving dish, topped with a knob of butter and a little washed, scissor-snipped parsley. Or grease a baking tray well, and pile the potatoes onto it in evenly-sized heaps. Fork them into castles, top with butter and either brown under a hot grill for a minute or two, or cook in a hot oven 200°C/400°F/gas 6–7 for 5 minutes until crisp and golden.

Cheesy – prepare creamed potatoes as above, beating 1–2 oz/25–50g grated cheese into the potato with the butter. Use as a topping for pies and savoury dishes, or pile onto a greased oven-proof dish, fork down evenly and top with a little more grated cheese. Brown under a hot grill for a minute or two, or put into a hot oven, 200°C/400°F/gas 6–7 for 5–10 minutes, until golden.

NEW POTATOES – lovely and easy, no peeling, but not much use as a mashed topping as they hold their shape and do not mash down very easily. You can use cooked new potatoes to make a topping, by slicing them thinly and arranging a thick layer of potato slices over a savoury filling or vegetable hot pot, dotting with butter and baking in a hot oven, 200°C/400°F/gas 6–7 for 15–20 minutes, until golden and crispy.

Allow 3–6 new potatoes per serving, according to size and appetite. Wash the potatoes well under running water, and scrub them with a pan scrubber or brush. (If you must, scrape them with a vegetable knife, but they have more flavour and goodness if cooked in their skins.) Put potatoes into a saucepan, cover with boiling water, add salt and a sprig of mint. Bring to the boil, lower heat and simmer for 15–20 minutes until tender. Drain well, tip into a dish and top with a knob of butter.

JACKET POTATOES

The ubiquitous favourite standby!

Heat oven – 200°C/400°F/gas 6–7.

Allow 1 medium or large potato per person.

Choose potatoes that do not have any mouldy-looking patches on the skin. Remember that very large spuds will take ages to cook, so if you're really hungry it may be better to cook 2 medium-sized potatoes.

Wash and scrub potato, *prick it several times with a fork*, and bake in one of the following ways:

Traditional Way: Put potato in the oven for 1–1½ hours according to size. The skin should be crisp and the inside soft and fluffy when ready. If you prefer softer potato skin, or don't want to risk the potato bursting all over the oven, wrap spud loosely in cooking foil before baking.

Quicker Way (1): Put the potato into a saucepan, cover well with hot water, bring to the boil and cook for 5–10 minutes according to size. Drain pan carefully, lift potato out with a cloth (*it will be very hot!*) and put it into the hot oven for 30–60 minutes according to size, until it feels soft.

Quicker Way (2): You can buy a "potato baker" in most cookware shops. This is a spiked stand on which you spear the potato before putting the whole thing into the oven. The cooking time is then halved, as the metal conducts the heat into the middle of the potato.

If you're cooking a casserole or a bake in the oven at a lower temperature, put the potato in the oven on the top shelf, with the casserole or bake lower down, and allow extra cooking time for the potato.

"Instant" Luxury Way: Cook *well-pricked* potato on kitchen paper in a microwave, according to manufacturer's instructions. We find that the skin of microwaved potatoes is rather soft and damp, not nice and crispy, so if there is time microwave potatoes for half the recommended time on each side, then holding potato in a cloth (it's hot!) transfer it to a hot, traditional oven, 200°C/400°F/gas 6–7, for 15–30 minutes according to size, until potato feels soft inside and crispy outside.

If you're really desperate, a tall, blond guy I know who is always starving, microwaves his jacket potatoes until completely cooked, then toasts them under a hot grill for a minute or two, turning them over to brown all the sides.

BAKED STUFFED POTATO

This can be prepared in advance and left in the fridge ready to heat through in a few minutes when needed.

Scrub and bake jacket potatoes (see page 65). When spud is soft, cut it carefully in half lengthways. Scoop out the soft potato into a bowl and mash with a fork adding a knob of butter ($\frac{1}{2}$ oz/12g) or 1 tblsp yoghurt for each potato. Add any of the fillings listed opposite and mix into the potato. Pile filling back into potato shell, and fork down evenly (it will be piled up well above the potato skin).

Place potato halves carefully on a baking tin or ovenproof dish. Sprinkle with a little grated cheese (optional, but it gives a lovely crispy topping) and either brown under a hot grill for a few minutes (don't have the grid too high up or the topping will burn before the potato is heated) or reheat the cold potato thoroughly in a hot oven, 200°C/400°F/gas 6–7 for 5–15 minutes, according to size, until golden brown.

If using microwaved baked potatoes, crisp the skin (see page 66) before cutting in half, or the shells will be too soft and may collapse.

A Few Filling Ideas

Prepare and cook jacket spud. When soft, put onto a warm plate, split open and top with your chosen filling and a knob of butter or tblsp yoghurt. These fillings are also good in pancakes – see page 30.

Cheese – 1–2 oz/25–50g grated Cheddar or Edam cheese.

Cheese & chives – Add handful of washed, scissor-snipped chives.

Cheese & pickle – Add 1 heaped tsp pickle or chutney.

Cheese & pineapple – Add 1–2 slices pineapple, chopped.

Cheese & sweetcorn – Add 1–2 tblsp canned or cooked sweetcorn.

Cottage cheese – 2–3 tblsp cottage cheese (plain or with chives, pineapple etc). Cottage cheese is also good with any of the above suggestions for grated cheese.

Baked beans – Heat the contents of a small tin of beans and pour over potato.

Bolognese – Top with Bolognese sauce (see page 61). A good way of using up any sauce left over from spaghetti.

Egg – Top potato with a fried egg, scrambled egg, omelette or fill with a hard-boiled egg, peeled and mashed with 1 tblsp mayonnaise (see page 181).

CHEESY SCALLOPED POTATOES

Serves 1–2

A substantial accompaniment to cutlets, burgers and nut roasts; or be generous with the cheese topping and eat it on its own for supper with a crispy green salad. If you make this dish in a larger quantity, increase the cooking time to $1\frac{1}{2}$ hours.

Preparation and cooking time: 50–60 minutes.

2–3 potatoes
1 small onion
Pinch of garlic powder
Salt, pepper
$\frac{1}{2}$ tsp mixed herbs
$\frac{1}{2}$ vegetable stock cube or $\frac{1}{2}$ tsp vegetable extract
$\frac{1}{4}$ pt/142ml/1 cup boiling water
1 tomato
1 oz/25g Cheddar or Edam cheese

Heat oven – 180°C/350°F/gas 4–5.
    Peel and thinly slice potatoes, peel and slice onion.
    Grease a deep, oven-proof dish and put in alternate layers of sliced potatoes and sliced onion, seasoning between each layer with garlic powder, salt, pepper and herbs.
    Dissolve stock cube or vegetable extract in boiling water and pour over the vegetables.
    Bake uncovered in the pre-heated oven for 40–45 minutes.
    Slice tomato and grate cheese.
    After about 30 minutes of the cooking time, arrange tomato slices on top of casserole and sprinkle with grated cheese. Return dish to the oven, and continue cooking until the stock is absorbed and the cheese is golden and bubbling.

KI'S POTATO FAVOURITE   *Serves 1–2*

Named after my youngest son, this is a nourishing, tasty
potato accompaniment to roasts or casseroles, which all the
family can enjoy.

Preparation and cooking time: 60 minutes.

2–3 potatoes
1 small onion
½ small green or red pepper
1 oz/25g Cheddar or Edam cheese – grated
1 tsp flour
Few sprigs of parsley and/or chives
Salt, pepper
¼ pt/142ml/1 cup milk
Little butter for topping

Heat oven – 200°C/400°F/gas 6–7.
  Grease a deep, oven-proof dish.
  Peel potatoes, cut into small dice (½"/1cm). Peel and chop
onion. Wash, slice and chop pepper. Mix vegetables together
in a bowl, stir in grated cheese, flour and washed scissor-
snipped herbs. Season well with salt and pepper. Turn
vegetable mixture into the well-greased dish. Heat milk and
pour over vegetable mixture. Dot top with dabs of butter,
and bake in the hot oven for about 45 minutes until the milk
is absorbed and the vegetables are cooked with a crispy top.
If top seems to be getting too brown, cover lightly with a
piece of cooking foil.

DAUPHIN POTATOES   *Serves 1–2*

This potato dish can be eaten on its own or with a salad or green vegetables as a supper dish, or served as a filling accompaniment to other dishes.

Preparation and cooking time: 1¼ hours.

1 clove of garlic
Little butter for greasing
2–3 potatoes
2 oz/50g Cheddar or Edam cheese (optional)
1 egg
¼ pt/142ml/1 cup milk
Salt, pepper
Pinch of nutmeg

Heat oven – 190°C/375°F/gas 5–6.

Peel garlic, cut clove in half and rub or press very hard over base and sides of an oven-proof dish. Discard crushed garlic and grease dish well with butter.

Peel and thinly slice potatoes. Grate cheese. Starting with potato, put alternate layers of potato slices and grated cheese into the buttered dish, ending with a sprinkle of cheese (if not using cheese, just put potato slices in the dish). Beat egg with a fork in a small basin, stir in milk, salt, pepper and nutmeg, and pour over potato.

Bake in the hot oven for about an hour, until potatoes are cooked and have a golden brown crust (cover with a loose lid of cooking foil if the top gets too brown).

WHOLEMEAL PASTRY (1)

Makes approximately 16 oz/450g pastry.

This dough can be used immediately after being made, and produces a light, crispy pastry.

Preparation time: 10 minutes.

6 oz/150g wholemeal plain flour
2 oz/50g white self-raising flour
4 oz/100g fat: use
    2 oz/50g butter or hard margarine
    2 oz/50g soft white cooking fat
    (a mixture of hard and soft fats gives the best result)
Pinch of salt
8 tsp cold water

Put flours into a mixing bowl, add fats cut into small pieces, and salt. Using finger tips, rub fat into flour until it looks like breadcrumbs – do not over rub as the soft fat melts easily. Gradually add cold water, mixing with a round bladed knife, and then forming a ball of dough using your hand. The pastry will be a bit soft and wet-looking, but should roll out satisfactorily on a lightly floured surface with a little more flour on the rolling pin.

  If you have naturally warm hands, cool your hands and wrists in cold running water, before making pastry, then the fat will not melt so quickly during rubbing-in.

WHOLEMEAL PASTRY (2)

Makes approximately 16 oz/450g pastry.

This pastry must be left in the fridge for at least half an hour or preferably overnight before use. Plain flour gives a crisper result; self-raising flour gives a more "cakey" pastry.

Preparation time: 10 minutes plus resting time.

8 oz/200g wholemeal flour – plain or self-raising
4 oz/100g soft cooking fat: use
    2 oz/50g soft margarine
    2 oz/50g soft white cooking fat
    (a mixture of the two fats gives the best colour and
    flavour)
Pinch of salt
3 tblsp cold water

Put about half the flour into a mixing bowl, add all the fat, salt and water and mix well with a fork – it will look like a cake mix. Add the rest of the flour and mix it in with the fork, then gradually mix together with your hand to form a wet dough – use a little extra flour on your hand if it seems to be very sticky – and knead gently into a ball.

Cover mixing bowl and leave pastry in the fridge for at least half an hour or overnight if possible.

BEANS, PEAS AND LENTILS

All pulses provide a good source of protein in the vegetarian diet. On average allow: 2 oz/50g dried beans per serving
4 oz/100g cooked or canned beans per serving

After cooking, the weight of dried beans will have doubled so do check whether the recipe is using dried or cooked beans.

6 oz/150g dried beans   = 15 oz/430g cooked/canned beans
1 heaped tblsp dried beans = 1 oz/25g dried beans
½ cup dried beans   = 3 oz/75g dried beans
1 cup cooked/canned beans   = 6 oz/150g approx.

If you generally use a small amount of beans, possibly only cooking for one vegetarian member of the family (until the next one is converted!), it is probably much easier, and not much more expensive, to buy canned beans which are ready cooked and just have to be added to the recipe when required (but remember to double the weight if using cooked beans and the recipe gives the quantity in dried beans). If you decide to use dried beans and you have a freezer available, it makes sense to cook a larger quantity and then freeze individual portions, to be defrosted and used in future dishes. A pressure cooker is excellent for cooking dried beans, and shortens the cooking time considerably if you follow the manufacturer's instructions carefully.

Beans vary tremendously in colour and size, but most mix together quite happily in stews or salads. Some of the most well-known ones which are widely available (dry or canned) are listed below; try these first and then experiment with the more unusual ones.

Red Beans: these beans *must always* be boiled hard for the first 10 minutes of their cooking time, to get rid of the toxins. (Canned beans have been boiled and are ready to use; they can just be heated through in stews, or eaten cold in salads.)

Red kidney beans – deep red, medium-size beans; use in salads, stews or chilli-type dishes.

Aduki beans – like little red kidney beans; very good in stews or mixed into savoury sauces.

White Beans: to be on the safe side, boil these hard for the first 5–10 minutes of cooking time, according to size (the larger the beans, the longer the cooking).

Butter beans – very large, creamy-coloured beans; good in vegetable stews and spicy dishes.

Barlotti beans – a medium size, pale brown bean; useful in

stews or casseroles.

Cannellini beans – white kidney beans, similar in size and texture to the red kidney bean, and can be substituted for them in recipes.

Haricot beans – probably best known in the commercial form as the popular "baked beans". Good in stews or salads.

Full Medam beans – I had to include these, as when we lived in the Middle East one manufacturer labelled his cans as containing "Foul Madams". I never plucked up courage to buy any! They are a beige-coloured medium-size bean, more widely available canned than dry. Use in stews or casseroles.

Flageolet beans – a bit smaller than kidney beans, a very pretty pale green colour. Give a lovely flavour to salads, mixed with other types of beans.

Chick peas – can be used in salads or stews, and mix well in cheesy dishes. They can be liquidised and used to make hummus, the popular Middle Eastern dip.

Dried peas – readily available in most supermarkets. They are generally soaked and used for soups or "mushy peas".

Split peas – "shelled peas", available in green or yellow varieties. Can be cooked without soaking and used in soups, stews, salads or to make pease pudding.

Whole lentils – available in various sizes and shades of

brown, beige and green. They can be cooked without pre-soaking and make good burgers, or they can be cooked with onion, herbs and spices to serve with rice or vegetables.

Split red lentils – "shelled" lentils, familiar for their lovely bright orange colour on the supermarket shelves. Can be cooked without soaking and used for soups, or to thicken stews and casseroles, to make spicy dhal to serve with curries, or for tasty burgers.

Canned beans are ready cooked. They just need to be drained, rinsed in a sieve or colander, and added to stews or casseroles, or mixed cold into salads.

Dried beans should be washed well before soaking and cooking, to remove dust and grit which may be found in them. Most dried beans (except for lentils and split peas) must be soaked before cooking, then rinsed in cold, running water before cooking in boiling UNSALTED water for between 20–90 minutes. The first 5–10 minutes of cooking time must be a really rapid boil, to get rid of any toxins present in the beans. This fast boil is *absolutely essential* in red kidney beans and aduki beans, to destroy completely the toxins they contain. Once this is done, they are completely safe and delicious to eat.

Do not add salt when soaking or boiling beans, it makes them tough. Seasonings should be added after cooking.

To soak dried beans – choose the most convenient of the following ways. Always wash beans well in cold water before soaking.

1.   Put rinsed beans in a large saucepan, half fill pan with cold water and soak for at least 8 hours or overnight.

2.   Put rinsed beans in a large saucepan, cover with boiling water and leave to soak for 1–2 hours.

3.   Put rinsed beans in a large saucepan, cover well with cold water and bring to the boil – turn off heat and leave to soak for ½–1 hour.

After soaking, the beans are ready for cooking. Do remember it is particularly important that red kidney and aduki beans are boiled hard for the first 10 minutes of the cooking time.

To cook soaked beans – drain beans well, put into a sieve or colander and rinse well again in cold water, then put beans into a large saucepan half full of cold water (remember do not add salt to the water) bring rapidly to the boil and allow to boil hard for at least 5 minutes (red kidney and aduki beans need 10 minutes), then lower heat and cook more slowly for 20–90 minutes until tender, generally the larger the beans the longer the cooking time.

If cooking beans in a pressure cooker, boil hard for 5–10 minutes then follow the manufacturer's instructions. Beans can also be cooked in a slow cooker, providing they are first boiled rapidly in a large saucepan for 5–10 minutes, then put into the slow cooker and cooked according to the manufacturer's instructions.

Approximate cooking times – most packets of dried beans will give recommended cooking times on the labels. Times will vary according to method and length of soaking beans.

Red kidney beans	– 45–60 minutes
Aduki beans	– 30–45 minutes
Butter beans	– 60–75 minutes
Barlotti beans	– 60–75 minutes
Cannellini beans	– 60–90 minutes

Haricot beans   – 60–75 minutes
Flageolet beans   – 45–60 minutes
Chick peas   – 45–60 minutes
Whole dried peas   – 45–60 minutes
Split peas   – 35–45 minutes
Whole lentils   – 45–60 minutes
Split red lentils – 20–30 minutes

Cook until tender. The beans are now ready to be used in the same way as canned beans in stews, casseroles, salads, burgers or dips, and can be seasoned with salt, herbs and spices.

Beans, Peas and Lentils – Family Meals

You'll find plenty of stews or casseroles in this section, as pulses (beans, peas and lentils) are at their most delicious cooked in a lovely rich gravy.

Most of the recipes in this section are for two people (just make double if you want a real family meal) as it's difficult making a stew in tiny amounts, especially if you want to include several different types of vegetables; also the gravy tends to dry up before the vegetables are cooked. The same assortment of vegetables can be used for both meat and vegetable casseroles, so prepare enough for the whole family and cook them in two separate dishes or pans (don't forget to use separate spoons as well, or there will be howls of protest if your vegetarian sees it!).

Canned beans are cooked, ready to drain and use, and are handy if you're only cooking vegetarian food for one or only need a small amount, but it is cheaper to use dried beans which can be cooked in larger quantities and kept in individual portions in the freezer.

Once the pulses have been cooked (or you have opened the can!) the actual vegetable stew or casserole is quickly prepared, as it only needs the time required for the vegetables to cook. In Winter, when stews are a popular and frequent family meal, I cheat a bit and save time by cooking double or treble quantities of stewing steak (without the veg) which I then freeze in portions suitable for the family. When next making a casserole meal, I prepare enough vegetables for everyone, add a portion of cooked, defrosted meat to the family dish, a portion of beans to the vegetarian dish and have both a meat and vegetarian casserole ready to eat in thirty minutes or so.

VEGETABLE AND BEAN STEW OR CASSEROLE

2–3 large helpings

You can use any mixture of veg and beans to make a casserole (cooked in the oven) or stew (simmered on top of the stove) so just use the veg you like or the ones that are available. If you are adding beans, these can be cooked beforehand, or use canned beans which are ready to cook with the vegetables.

Preparation and cooking time: 1 hour (plus time to soak and cook dried beans).

4 oz/100g/just over ½ cup dried beans – kidney, aduki, barlotti, lentils etc.
or
1 small (7 oz/230g) can beans   *(continued overleaf)*

(Vegetable and Bean Stew or Casserole continued)

1 onion, peeled and sliced
2 sticks of celery, washed and cut into 1″/2½cm lengths
1 clove of garlic, peeled and chopped or ¼ tsp mixed garlic
1 carrot, peeled and sliced
1 piece of swede, peeled thickly, cut into chunks
1 very small turnip, peeled thickly, cut into chunks
1 parsnip, peeled and cut into chunks
1 potato, peeled and cut into chunks
1 courgette, washed and thickly sliced
1 very small aubergine, washed and thickly sliced
½ green pepper, washed, seeds removed and sliced
Few mushrooms, washed and sliced if large
2–3 large tomatoes, washed and sliced
or 1 small (7 oz/230g) can tomatoes
1 tblsp cooking oil
1 tsp flour or cornflour, for thickening gravy
1 vegetable stock cube
½ tsp yeast extract
1 cup/¼ pt/142ml water and/or beer
½ glass of wine or sherry (optional)
Salt, pepper
½ tsp herbs
Dash of Worcester sauce

Soak and cook dried beans if used (see page 76). Make sure
kidney and aduki beans (if used) are fast boiled for the first
10 minutes of their cooking time, otherwise they could be
poisonous.

Prepare all the vegetables.

Heat oil in saucepan or casserole and gently fry onion,
celery and garlic for 4–5 minutes, over a medium heat,
stirring well.

Add root vegetables and continue to fry gently for 2–3 minutes, then add remaining vegetables.

Mix flour, stock cube and yeast extract to a smooth paste with alcohol or a little cold water, add rest of water and stir into vegetable mixture. Add cooked beans or drained canned beans and seasoning, herbs and Worcester sauce.

Bring gently to the boil, stir and put the covered casserole dish into a moderate oven – 170°C/325°F/gas 3–4 or simmer over a very low heat, with the lid on, for 30–45 minutes, stirring occasionally, until all the vegetables are cooked.

RED STEW   *2 very generous helpings*

Not straight from the Kremlin, but probably suitable for the Russian weather. This lovely filling winter dish is best made in this larger quantity as very small amounts dry up during cooking, and you will have half an aubergine lying around.

Preparation and cooking time: 1 hour (plus cooking time for beans).

½ cup/3 oz/75g dried red kidney beans
or 1 cup/6 oz/150g cooked or canned red kidney beans
1 onion
1 clove garlic or ¼ tsp garlic powder
1 small aubergine
½ small red pepper
3–4 tomatoes, fresh or canned
1–2 tblsp vegetable oil and ½ oz/12g butter for frying
1 glass red wine (optional but nice)
2 tsp tomato purée or ketchup
1 vegetable stock cube   *(continued overleaf)*

(Red Stew continued)

1–2 cups/¼–½ pt/142–284ml water (use water from cooking dried beans or the liquid from canned beans)
Salt, pepper
½ tsp mixed herbs

Soak and cook dried beans if used (see page 76). Make sure that they boil hard for the first 10 minutes of the cooking time, otherwise they could be poisonous. Save the cooking liquid.

Peel and chop onion and fresh garlic. Wash and cut aubergine into bite-sized chunks. Wash, de-seed and chop pepper. Wash and chop fresh tomatoes.

Heat oil and butter in a saucepan or casserole pot over a medium heat, and fry onion and garlic for 3–4 minutes until soft. Add aubergine and continue to fry gently for a further 4–5 minutes, stirring carefully, and adding a little more oil if necessary. Add pepper and fry for a few more minutes, then add cooked beans, tomatoes and wine if used. Stir in tomato purée or ketchup, crumbled stock cube and 1 cup bean liquid or water, salt, pepper and herbs.

Bring to the boil, then lower heat, put lid on the pan and simmer very gently for 45 minutes, stirring occasionally and adding more liquid if needed as the stew cooks.

Serve with jacket potatoes or hot, crusty bread.

WHITE BEAN STEW   *2 generous servings*

Make at least enough for 2, as smaller amounts tend to dry up during cooking. You can cook your own dried beans or use cooked canned beans. Any white beans are fine for this recipe – butter, haricot, barlotti or cannellini beans for instance – but I like the large white butter beans best.

Preparation and cooking time: 45 minutes (plus soaking and cooking time for dried beans).

3 oz/75g/½ cup dried white beans – butter, haricot, cannellini, barlotti
or 6 oz/150g/1 cup cooked or canned white beans
1 onion
1 clove of garlic or ¼ tsp ground garlic
1 stick of celery
1 tblsp vegetable oil – olive oil gives this dish a nice flavour
8 oz/200g fresh tomatoes or small can (7 oz/230g) tomatoes
1 small green or red pepper
2 tsp tomato purée or ketchup
½ tsp dried mixed herbs
½ tsp sugar
Salt, pepper
1–2 tblsp plain yoghurt (optional)
Few sprigs of fresh parsley or chives

Soak dried beans, rinse well, then cook in plenty of boiling water for 1–1½ hours according to type – see page 76.

Peel and chop onion and fresh garlic. Wash and chop celery.

Heat oil in a saucepan or flame-proof casserole over a moderate heat and fry onion, garlic and celery for 5–6 minutes, until softened but not browned. Wash and chop fresh tomatoes, wash, de-seed and chop peppers and add both to onion mixture. Stir in tomato purée or ketchup, mixed herbs and sugar, and simmer gently for 10 minutes, stirring frequently.

Stir in cooked or drained canned beans, season to taste with salt and pepper, and simmer for a further 10 minutes until beans are thoroughly heated through in a nice, thick sauce.

Stir in yoghurt (if used) and sprinkle with washed, scissor-snipped parsley or chives.

Serve with jacket potatoes, rice, pasta or hot, crusty bread.

HOME-MADE BAKED BEANS   *Serves 2*

Quite a change from the canned varieties, very tasty and filling. It's easier to make at least two helpings of this casserole, as a very tiny amount tends to boil dry before the dish is cooked. You can use either pre-cooked dried beans or canned beans for this recipe, which can be cooked either in the oven or on the top of the stove over a very low heat.

Preparation and cooking time: 55–60 minutes plus soaking and cooking time for dried beans.

1 small onion
1 tblsp vegetable oil
7–8 oz/175–200g dried haricot beans, soaked and cooked for about 1 hour
or 15 oz/425g canned haricot beans
1 tblsp soft brown sugar
1 tsp black treacle or molasses
1 tsp made-up mustard
1 tblsp tomato purée or ketchup
½ cup/2½ fl oz/70ml bean liquid – save cooking water or liquid from the can

Salt, pepper
1–2 tsp lemon juice

Heat oven if necessary – 150°C/300°F/gas 2–3.

Peel and finely chop onion. Heat oil in a heavy saucepan
or casserole pot over a moderate heat and fry onion gently
for 5 minutes until softened. Drain cooked beans (save the
liquid) and stir gently into the onion. Mix in brown sugar,
treacle or molasses, mustard, tomato purée or ketchup and
about ½ cup of the bean liquid. Bring slowly to the boil, stir
well, cover and cook either in the low oven, or reduce the
heat and simmer very, very gently on top of the stove for
about 45 minutes, stirring occasionally until beans and sauce
are a good thick consistency.

Season to taste with salt, pepper and a little lemon juice.
Serve piping hot with jacket potatoes or hot, crusty rolls.

LENTIL AND VEGETABLE STEW

Serves 2–3

A very cheap, filling dish, super on a cold day served with
fresh green vegetables or a crunchy green salad. It is easier to
prepare enough for several people, as very small amounts
dry up during cooking.

Preparation and cooking time: 55 minutes.

4 oz/100g/just over ½ cup dried green lentils
1 small onion
1 clove of fresh garlic or ¼ tsp garlic granules
1 small leek
1–2 sticks of celery *(continued overleaf)*

(Lentil and Vegetable Stew continued)

1–2 courgettes or small piece of marrow (about 4 oz/100g)
1 small potato
1 tblsp vegetable oil
½ stock cube (vegetable) crumbled into ½ cup/2½ fl oz/70ml
**   water**
Salt, pepper
2 tsp lemon juice
Few sprigs of fresh parsley

Wash and drain lentils (no need to soak) and cook in about ½ pt/284ml/2 cups boiling water, until the water is partly absorbed and the lentils are becoming tender – about 30 minutes.

Peel and chop onion and fresh garlic. Trim and wash leek very thoroughly to remove any grit, and slice into rings. Trim, wash and chop celery. Top, tail, wash and slice courgettes or peel and cube marrow. Peel and cut potato into 1″/2½cm dice.

Heat oil in a flame-proof casserole or heavy saucepan over a moderate heat, and fry onion, garlic, leek and celery for 5–6 minutes, until softened but not brown. Add half-cooked lentils, courgette or marrow and potato cubes. Add the crumbled stock cube and water, and continue to simmer for a further 15–20 minutes, until the vegetables are cooked. Most of the liquid will be absorbed during cooking, just leaving a little gravy. Season to taste with salt, pepper, lemon juice and washed scissor-snipped parsley.

DHAL   *2 generous helpings*

A spicy "saucy" dish, often served with curry dishes or

boiled rice. It makes a tasty meal as an accompaniment to winter vegetables or a very nourishing sauce with burgers or roasts.

Preparation and cooking time: 35–40 minutes.

1 small onion
1 clove of garlic or $\frac{1}{4}$ tsp ground garlic
1 tblsp vegetable oil
4 oz/100g/$\frac{1}{2}$ generous cup dried split red lentils
1 tsp ground cumin
1 tsp ground turmeric
1 tsp ground coriander
$\frac{1}{2}$ tsp ground cinnamon
$\frac{1}{4}$ tsp chilli powder (optional)
$\frac{3}{4}$ pt/426ml/3 cups water
Salt, pepper
1 tsp lemon juice

Peel and finely chop onion and fresh garlic. Heat oil in a saucepan over a medium heat and fry onion and garlic for 5 minutes until soft but not brown.

Add washed, drained lentils, spices and water and bring slowly to the boil, stirring occasionally, then reduce heat, and simmer very gently for 20–25 minutes, until the water is almost absorbed and the lentils are tender (watch the pan carefully for the last few minutes to make sure the lentils do not boil dry and burn). When the last spoonful of water is absorbed the lentils will have a thick paste-like consistency.

Season dhal to taste with salt, pepper and lemon juice and serve hot or cold.

VEGETABLE DISHES

Lots of these dishes can make a meal in themselves, or if served as an accompaniment they can be enjoyed with other vegetarian dishes or served to the non-converted members of the family with meat dishes.

Now is the time to experiment with some of the different vegetables and fruits that are appearing in the supermarkets and greengrocers' shops. Often recipe sheets and ways of cooking new vegetables are available where they are sold. In this section you may find recipes for vegetables you have not cooked before.

RATATOUILLE *2 generous helpings*

"Ratts" as this is called by one member of our family, is really a delicious vegetable mixture with a Mediterranean flavour. The best and traditional flavour is obtained by using a good olive oil, but any vegetable oil can be used and is generally cheaper. Because you need a mixture of vegetables it is more economical to make a larger amount (why not try double the quantity given in this recipe?) Ratatouille can be eaten cold or hot, and it freezes well in individual plastic containers. It is an interesting accompaniment to nut or lentil roast, burgers etc., (or to grilled or roast meat dishes for the non-converted!) or it can be eaten on its own as a light lunch, sprinkled with the traditional Greek Feta cheese.

Preparation and cooking time: 30 minutes.

1 onion
1 clove of garlic or $\frac{1}{4}$ tsp garlic granules
1 small aubergine
1–2 courgettes
$\frac{1}{2}$ red pepper
$\frac{1}{2}$ green pepper
2 tomatoes – fresh, or drained canned ones
2–3 tblsp olive oil or vegetable oil
Salt, pepper
1 tsp mixed herbs
Few sprigs of fresh parsley

Peel and slice onion, peel and chop fresh garlic. Wash and slice aubergine ($\frac{1}{2}$ inch/1cm thick); there is no need to salt and drain the aubergine for this dish as any bitterness is masked by the general flavourings. Wash and slice courgettes, wash peppers, remove seeds and slice. Wash and thickly slice tomatoes.

Heat chosen oil in a medium-size saucepan, over a moderate heat and fry onion and garlic for 4–5 minutes until softened but not brown. Add sliced aubergine, courgettes and peppers, stirring carefully into the oil, but try not to break up the vegetables. Continue frying gently and stir in tomatoes, salt, pepper and herbs and simmer for 7–10 minutes, stirring occasionally until the vegetables are cooked but not mushy.

Turn into a warmed serving dish, and garnish with washed, scissor-snipped parsley and serve hot, or allow to cool and chill in the fridge if to be served cold.

SAVOURY MUSHROOM PIE   *Serves 1*

A tasty potato-topped dinner or supper dish.

Preparation and cooking time: 45 minutes.

2 potatoes – medium-size (more or less according to appetite)
Salt, pepper
1 onion
1 clove of garlic or ¼ tsp garlic powder
1 stick of celery
4 oz/100g mushrooms
½ oz/12g butter
1 oz/25g grated Cheddar or Edam cheese
1 tblsp vegetable oil
1 tsp flour or cornflour
½ cup/2½ fl oz/70ml milk
2 tblsp cashew nuts or pine nuts kernels
½ tsp mixed herbs
Few sprigs of parsley
½ tsp lemon juice
1 tomato, sliced for decoration

Peel potatoes, cut into thick slices and cook in boiling salted water for 8–10 minutes, until potatoes feel soft when tested with a knife.

Peel and slice onion and fresh garlic. Wash and chop celery. Wash and slice mushrooms.

Drain potatoes when cooked, then mash with a potato masher or fork and wooden spoon. Beat in butter and grated cheese and season with salt and pepper. Leave in pan with lid on.

Heat oil in a saucepan over a medium heat and fry onion, celery and garlic gently for 4–5 minutes until soft. Add mushrooms and continue to cook gently for 3–4 minutes, stirring occasionally.

Mix flour or cornflour to a smooth paste with 1 tblsp of the milk, stir in rest of milk and pour it all into the mushroom mixture, stirring over a low heat until sauce thickens. Add nuts, herbs and washed, scissor-snipped parsley, lemon juice, salt and pepper and simmer for a further 2–3 minutes, stirring gently.

Put vegetable mixture into an individual pie dish. Top with the cheesy potato and fork the top decoratively. Garnish with tomato slices and brown under a hot grill until golden brown.

This pie can be made in advance and kept in the fridge or frozen until needed. It is then best to heat it through thoroughly in a moderate oven – 180°C/350°F/gas 4–5 for 10–15 minutes, until hot and golden brown on top.

MUSHROOMS À LA GREQUE

Serves 2 or 1 hungry person

This is really a vegetable accompaniment, not a main meal,

although it would make a delicious snack or light lunch. It goes well with nut roast, lentil roast, vegeburgers, soya pie, etc.

Preparation and cooking time: 30 minutes.

4 oz/100g mushrooms
1 small onion
1 clove of garlic or $\frac{1}{4}$ tsp minced garlic
1 tblsp olive oil or vegetable oil
$\frac{1}{2}$ vegetable stock cube
$\frac{1}{2}$ cup/2$\frac{1}{2}$ fl oz/70ml boiling water
$\frac{1}{4}$ tsp vegetable extract
1 tblsp white wine or cider
2 tsp tomato purée or ketchup
$\frac{1}{2}$ tsp mixed herbs
Salt, pepper
Few sprigs of fresh parsley or chives
Paprika or cayenne pepper for garnish

Heat oven – 170°C/325°F/gas 3–4.

Wash and thickly slice mushrooms (leave tiny button mushrooms whole) and put into a casserole dish. Peel and slice onion and garlic. Heat oil in saucepan, over a gentle heat and fry onion and garlic for 4–5 minutes until softened. Spoon this over mushrooms.

Dissolve stock cube in the boiling water, add vegetable extract, wine or cider, tomato purée or ketchup, and pour over vegetables.

Sprinkle with mixed herbs, season to taste with salt and pepper. Wash and scissor-snip parsley or chives over the dish.

Bake in the hot oven for 15–20 minutes, until the mushrooms are soft.

Sprinkle with paprika or cayenne, depending on whether you like it hot, and serve.

OKRA (LADIES' FINGERS)

1 very generous helping

Try this more unusual vegetable as a light lunch or supper dish, served with rice or warm pitta bread, or use it as a tasty accompaniment to roasts or burgers.

Preparation and cooking time: 35–45 minutes.

4 oz/100g fresh okra
1 small onion
1 clove of garlic or $\frac{1}{4}$ tsp garlic granules
1–2 tomatoes, fresh or canned
1–2 tblsp vegetable oil
1 tsp tomato purée or ketchup
Salt, pepper
$\frac{1}{4}$ tsp sugar
$\frac{1}{2}$ tsp mixed herbs or ground coriander
1 tsp lemon juice
Approximately $\frac{1}{2}$ cup/$2\frac{1}{2}$ fl oz/70ml cold water or juice from canned tomatoes.

Top and tail okra, rinse in cold water. Peel and slice onion, peel and finely chop fresh garlic, wash and chop fresh tomatoes. Heat oil in a pan over a moderate heat, and fry onion and garlic gently for 3–4 minutes, until softened but not browned. Add okra, and continue to cook gently for a further 4–5 minutes, until beginning to soften. Add chopped tomatoes, tomato purée or ketchup, salt, pepper, sugar, herbs and lemon juice. Add about $\frac{1}{2}$ cup water or tomato juice, just enough to half cover the vegetables in the pan, and simmer until the okra is tender, about 20–30 minutes.

Taste sauce and adjust seasoning if necessary. Serve hot or cold (but I prefer it hot).

CRISPY CABBAGE CASSEROLE

Serves 1–2

This is filling enough to serve as a cheap supper dish on its own, with hot bread rolls and butter. It is also delicious as an accompaniment but is very filling.

Preparation and cooking time: 35 minutes.

1 portion of hard white cabbage (or quarter of a small cabbage)
1 small onion
1–2 sticks of celery
1 tblsp vegetable oil
1 thick slice brown bread
Large knob of butter

Cheese sauce
2 tsp flour or cornflour
1 cup/¼ pt milk
½ oz/12g butter or margarine
1–2 oz/25–50g Cheddar or Edam cheese
Salt, pepper
Pinch of mustard

Heat oven – 200°C/400°F/gas 6–7.
    Grease a deep oven-proof dish or casserole. Trim outer leaves and stalk from the cabbage. Shred cabbage, not too finely, wash well and drain. Peel and chop onion. Scrape,

wash and cut celery into 1″/2½cm lengths. Heat oil in a large frying pan, and fry onion gently for 2–3 minutes, until softened. Add celery and drained cabbage and fry gently for 5 minutes, stirring occasionally.

Make the cheese sauce – see page 176. Put the vegetable mixture into the greased dish, and pour the cheese sauce over the top.

Crumble the bread into crumbs using a liquidiser or grater and sprinkle these thickly on top of the sauce. Dot with flakes of butter and bake, uncovered, in the hot oven for 15–20 minutes, until the top is crunchy and golden brown.

RED CABBAGE SAVOURY

Serves 2–3

A warming vegetable dish, good with jacket potatoes on a Winter's day or as an accompaniment to roasts or grills. Can be cooked on top of the stove or in the oven.

Preparation and cooking time: 1 hour.

1 small onion
½ small red cabbage
1 eating apple
1 tblsp vegetable oil
2–3 tblsp salted peanuts or cashew nuts
Salt, pepper
2 tsp sugar – brown if possible
2 tsp vinegar
½ cup/2½ fl oz/70ml boiling water

Heat oven, if being used – 180°C/350°F/gas 4–5.

Peel and chop onion. Cut stalk from cabbage and remove any battered outside leaves. Shred cabbage, wash and drain. Peel, core and slice apple. Heat oil in a pan over a moderate heat and fry onion for 2–3 minutes until softened but not brown.

Pan Method

In a heavy saucepan, put layers of cabbage, apple, onion and nuts, seasoning each layer with salt, pepper, sugar and vinegar. Pour ½ cup boiling water over it, and top with a sprinkle of sugar. Put on saucepan lid and simmer gently for 35–45 minutes, stirring occasionally, until the vegetables are cooked. Watch to make sure that the vegetables don't burn towards the end of the cooking time.

Oven Method

Use a casserole dish with a lid. Put the vegetables in layers, as in the pan method, adding the ½ cup boiling water and sugar. Cook in the hot oven, stirring occasionally, for about 45 minutes.

Jacket potatoes can be cooked in the oven with the casserole.

PIPERADE STUFFED COURGETTES

1–2 servings

Use good-sized, even-shaped courgettes for this dish, which can be served as a starter for two or a generous main course for one person.

Preparation and cooking time: 30–35 minutes.

1–2 medium-size courgettes
Salt, pepper
½ small onion
½ small green or red pepper
1–2 tomatoes, fresh or canned
1 tblsp vegetable oil
Pinch of garlic powder
2 eggs
Few sprigs of fresh parsley

Trim and wash courgettes, and cook whole in gently boiling salted water for 6–7 minutes, until just soft (test by pricking with a fork). Drain courgettes, and leave in the saucepan with the lid on while you prepare the piperade.

Make piperade – peel and slice onion, wash core and chop pepper. Wash and chop tomatoes. Heat oil in a saucepan and cook onion and pepper over a medium heat stirring well until soft, 4–5 minutes. Add chopped tomatoes, garlic, salt and pepper and stir. Continue to cook gently over a low heat, stirring occasionally for about 15 minutes, to make a thick saucy mixture.

Break eggs into a small basin and lightly beat them with a fork, ready to cook.

Remove courgettes from pan, split them in half lengthways and hollow out the seedy, centre part leaving a thick courgette shell. Put on a serving dish and keep warm while cooking the egg.

Pour the beaten egg into the vegetable mixture, stirring hard with a wooden spoon over a low heat until eggs are just setting (do not over-cook or the eggs will go hard instead of soft and creamy). Spoon filling into prepared courgette halves. Eat hot or cold as preferred.

COURGETTE AND CHICK PEA GRATINÉ

Serves 1

Use canned, ready cooked chick peas for this recipe unless
you have some left-over cooked chick peas to use up.

Preparation and cooking time: 30 minutes.

1 courgette
Salt
1 small onion
2 tsp vegetable oil for frying
½ cup/3 oz/75g canned or cooked chick peas
1 heaped tblsp nuts – peanuts, cashew nuts or pine kernels
Salt, pepper
1–2 oz/25g–50g grated cheese (Cheddar and/or Parmesan)

White Sauce
1 level tsp flour or cornflour
¼ cup/1½ fl oz/45ml milk
Dab of butter

Wash and slice (½ inch/1cm) or cube courgette. Simmer
gently in salted water for 2–5 minutes until just tender. Drain
very well as they tend to be a bit watery (shake drained pan
over a very low heat for a few minutes to get them really dry).

Peel and finely chop onion, heat oil in saucepan over a low
heat and fry onion gently for 3–4 minutes until soft, stirring
occasionally. Remove from heat.

Put flour or cornflour into a cup or small basin, mix into a
runny paste with 1 tblsp of the milk. Stir in the rest of the
milk, pour it all over the onion in the pan stirring well.
Return pan to heat and cook gently until sauce thickens,
stirring all the time, and beat in butter.

Add chick peas and nuts, then gently stir in the courgette, season well with salt and pepper and heat through over a low heat.

Tip into an oven-proof dish, top with the grated cheese (a mixture of Cheddar and Parmesan gives a nice flavour) and brown under a hot grill until bubbly and golden.

Serve with a salad as a light lunch or supper, or with a jacket potato and vegetables as a more substantial meal.

ITALIAN COURGETTES   *1 serving*

I think this is my favourite courgette recipe. It's delicious on its own as a light lunch or supper, or makes a nice saucy vegetable served with "dry" meals – roasts burgers, pasties etc.

Preparation and cooking time: 25 minutes.

1–2 courgettes
1 clove of garlic or $\frac{1}{4}$ tsp garlic powder
1 tblsp vegetable oil
1–2 tomatoes, fresh or canned
1 tsp lemon juice
Few sprigs of fresh parsley
Salt, pepper
1 tblsp vegetable oil with 1 oz/25g butter for frying
1–2 tblsp fresh wholemeal breadcrumbs
1 tblsp grated Parmesan cheese.

Trim courgettes and cut into $\frac{1}{2}$"/1cm slices. Peel and finely chop fresh garlic. Heat the first tablespoon of oil in a saucepan over a moderate heat, and cook courgettes and garlic gently for 3–4 minutes until tender, turning frequently.

Wash and chop tomatoes and add to courgette mixture. Continue to cook gently, for a further 3–4 minutes, stirring frequently, and adding lemon juice and washed scissor-snipped parsley. Season to taste with salt and pepper.

Heat remaining oil and butter in a clean frying pan over a moderate heat and fry breadcrumbs for a few minutes, stirring all the time, until crispy and golden.

Pour hot courgette mixture into a serving dish. Cover thickly with hot, crispy breadcrumbs and top with a sprinkle of grated Parmesan cheese. Serve at once.

STUFFED PEPPER   *1 pepper*

You can use up left-over cooked rice for this dish. I always freeze any extra cooked rice in individual plastic containers, and it's quick to defrost when needed. You can easily make stuffed peppers for a family meal by varying the fillings to suit everybody.

Preparation and cooking time: 1¼ hours.

1 large green or red pepper

For each pepper allow:
2 oz/50g/2 tblsp cooked brown or white rice
or
1 oz/25g/1 tblsp dry rice
½ small onion
1 small tomato – fresh or canned
2 tsp vegetable oil
½ tsp mixed herbs
1 tsp pine kernels or chopped nuts
1 tsp seedless raisins or sultanas (optional)

Salt, pepper, ½ tsp yeast extract
1 tsp tomato purée or ketchup
½ cup/2½ fl oz/70ml (approx) juice from canned tomatoes, tomato soup or water with ¼ crumbled vegetable stock cube

Heat oven – 180°C/350°F/gas 4–5.

Cook dry rice if used (see page 48).

Peel and finely chop onion. Wash and chop fresh tomato. Heat oil in a small saucepan over a moderate heat and fry onion gently for 2–3 minutes until just softened. Add chopped tomato and cook for a further minute. Stir in herbs, pine kernels or nuts, raisins or sultanas (if used) and cooked rice. Season with salt and pepper and a little yeast extract.

Wash pepper, slice top off and remove seeds (keep the top). Fill pepper with the prepared stuffing, replace the top, and stand in a small deep oven-proof dish. Mix tomato purée with chosen liquid (crumble stock cube into boiling water and stir to dissolve if used), and pour liquid carefully into the dish, so that the pepper is standing in the liquid. Cover dish with a lid or piece of cooking foil and bake in the moderate oven for about an hour, until the pepper is soft. Serve hot or cold with any remaining sauce poured over the top.

ITALIAN-STYLE STEWED PEPPERS

1 generous helping

This is a filling vegetable dish, providing both vegetables and a sauce to go with nut roasts, lentil cutlets etc. (or roast or grilled meat for non-vegetarians), and is tasty poured over cooked spaghetti. The price of peppers varies tremendously according to the season, so if you have a freezer make a larger quantity of the recipe when they're cheap and store for future use. Also, if you make a larger amount, enough for

3–4 servings, you can use different coloured peppers, which makes a most attractive dish.

Preparation and cooking time: 30 minutes.

1 small onion
1 clove of garlic or ¼ tsp minced garlic
1 medium-sized tomato
1 pepper – red, green or yellow
1 tblsp oil (olive oil gives the best, traditional flavour, but any
       vegetable oil can be used)
Salt, pepper
½ tsp mixed herbs, dried or freshly chopped

Peel and slice onion, peel and chop fresh garlic, wash and roughly chop tomato, wash, core and slice pepper in rings or chunks.

Heat oil in a pan over a medium heat and fry onion and garlic gently for 3–5 minutes until softened but not browned. Add sliced pepper and fry gently for a further 5 minutes until softened, then add tomato and continue to simmer gently for a further 5–10 minutes until all the vegetables are cooked but not mushy (larger amounts may take a few minutes longer to cook). The mixture will thicken as it cooks.

Season with salt, pepper and herbs. Serve hot.

STUFFED CABBAGE PARCELS   *1 serving*

This makes an appetising meal for the whole family if you increase the quantities. If some people insist on being non-vegetarian, you could omit the nuts and substitute chopped cooked chicken or ham in their parcels.

Preparation and cooking time: 40–45 minutes.

Per person:
2 large green cabbage leaves
½ small onion
2–3 mushrooms
1 tblsp cooked rice – brown or white
2 tsp vegetable oil
1 tblsp cashew nuts or pine nut kernels
1 tblsp cooked or canned sweetcorn
Few drops of Worcester sauce and/or a little tabasco sauce
Salt, pepper
¼ pt/142ml/1 cup home-made tomato sauce – see page 178

Heat oven – 180°C/350°F/gas 4–5.

Wash and trim cabbage leaves. Blanch them by putting the leaves into a large saucepan, cover with boiling water and bring back to the boil for about 1 minute. This will make the leaves soft enough to bend without tearing. Drain carefully and put aside.

Peel and chop onion finely. Wash and slice mushrooms. Cook rice if you don't have any left-over ready cooked – see page 48.

Heat oil in a saucepan over a moderate heat and fry onion gently for 2–3 minutes until soft but not brown. Add mushrooms and cook for a further minute, then stir in nuts and sweetcorn. Season to taste with Worcester or a little tabasco sauce, salt and pepper.

Divide filling between prepared cabbage leaves and carefully fold into neat parcels (secure with wooden, not plastic, cocktail sticks if you have problems, but don't forget to remove them before serving!). Put parcels into a small casserole dish. Pour prepared tomato sauce over the top, cover with lid and cook in the moderate oven for 20–25 minutes.

The cabbage parcels are good served with roast or baked potatoes or plain boiled noodles.

SAVOURY APPLE SLICES   *Serves 2–4*

A very versatile, tasty savoury slice. Serve hot with vegetables or salad for lunch or supper, or cut into wedges when cold and take on a picnic or for a packed lunch. It is delicious, hot or cold, cut into fingers for party nibbles. Useful at Christmas time when a large slice (double the quantity of ingredients so that it fills a large Swiss roll tin) can be made and lightly baked in advance, deep frozen ready to defrost and reheat when needed.

Preparation and cooking time: 45 minutes.

1 quantity of vege sausages (using 4 oz/100g nuts) as given on page 154
½ x 13 oz/375g packet frozen puff pastry – defrosted
1 small cooking apple

Heat oven – 200°C/400°F/gas 6–7.
Prepare vege sausage mixture, adding a little more beaten egg if necessary to make a firm spreading consistency. Keep the remaining egg for brushing the pastry later. Save one quarter of the pastry, and roll out the remainder into an oblong approximately 9″ x 6″/23cm x 15cm. Lift pastry over a floured rolling pin and place on a baking sheet. Roll out remaining pastry thinly, ⅛″/¼cm, and cut into strips ½″/1cm wide.
Spread vege sausage mixture over the pastry oblong, leaving a narrow margin, ¼″/½cm all round the edges.
Peel, core and thinly slice the cooking apple, and arrange

the apple slices neatly over the vege sausage. Make a trellis over the top with the pastry strips, sticking the edges of the pastry firmly by moistening with a little cold water.

Brush the pastry trellis and the pastry edges with the beaten egg. Bake for 15–20 minutes in the hot oven, until the pastry is well risen and golden.

VEGETARIAN KEBABS   *2–4 Kebabs*

A tasty vegetable kebab, easily prepared with the more usual meat kebabs, so that the vegetarian need not miss out at the barbeque (but marinate the vegetable kebabs in a separate dish away from the meat kebabs and cook on the far side of the barbeque, away from the meat!). Use any mixture of the suggested vegetables.

Preparation and cooking time: 25 minutes. Plus 30 minutes draining aubergine slices and 1 hour marinating kebabs.

½ small aubergine
1 small courgette
6 button mushrooms
4 shallots or 1 onion
2 strips of red pepper – about 1"/2½cm wide
2 strips of green pepper – about 1"/2½cm wide
1 large or 2 small tomatoes

Marinade
1 clove of garlic or ¼ tsp minced garlic
1 tblsp vegetable oil (olive and walnut have the best flavour)
1 tblsp soy sauce
1 tsp Worcester sauce   *(continued overleaf)*

(Vegetarian Kebabs continued)

1 tblsp sugar – brown or white
1 tsp whole grain mustard
Salt, pepper

Keep the vegetables in separate heaps when you have prepared them. Wash aubergine, cut into bite-sized chunks about $\frac{1}{2}$″/1cm thick, put pieces in a colander and sprinkle with salt. Stand colander on a plate to catch the bitter juices which will drain out and leave to drain for about 30 minutes. Rinse and dry.

Trim and wash courgette, cut in 1″/2$\frac{1}{2}$cm rings.

Wash mushrooms.

Peel shallots, or peel onion and cut into 4 chunks.

Wash pepper strips, cut into 1$\frac{1}{2}$″/3cm lengths.

Wash tomatoes, cut into quarters or halves.

Make up kebabs, by threading the vegetable pieces fairly tightly and evenly onto the skewers, mixing the different types of vegetables. Lie skewers flat in a deep dish or plastic container (china or Pyrex-type, not metal).

To make the marinade: peel, chop and crush fresh garlic, put into a small basin with the oil and mix well, pressing the garlic juices out, or mix in minced garlic. Stir in the other ingredients and mix well. Pour marinade over kebabs and leave for at least an hour, turning skewers and basting occasionally.

Grill kebabs on the barbeque grid or under a hot grill (not too close to the heat or they'll burn before the vegetables are cooked) for about 10 minutes.

Serve with rice or jacket potatoes and salads.

Any remaining marinade can be poured over cooked kebabs to make a tasty sauce.

PEASE PUDDING

Serves 3–4

Despite its "old-fashioned flat cap" image, pease pudding can be a tasty addition to a vegetarian meal. It is good served with nut roasts or vegeburgers, or as an accompaniment to stews or casseroles. It's hardly worth cooking very small amounts of the peas, so if possible make a family quantity and freeze any spare portions ready to defrost and cook when needed.

Preparation and cooking time: 45–50 minutes to cook peas
45 minutes to prepare and cook pudding.

8 oz/200g/1 full cup split peas – green or yellow
1 large onion
1 tblsp vegetable oil
1 egg
Salt, pepper
½ tsp sugar

Rinse split peas (no need to soak) and cook in large pan of boiling water for 45–50 minutes, until soft. Drain well.

Heat oven – 180°C/350°F/gas 4–5. Grease a deep pie dish or casserole.

Peel and chop onion, heat oil in a saucepan over a moderate heat and fry onion gently for 5 minutes, until quite soft but not browned. Mix onion into the peas. Beat egg in a small basin with salt, pepper and sugar, then pour egg into the pea mixture and beat together well to form a thick purée.

Spoon into the greased dish, cover with lid or a piece of cooking foil, and bake in the moderate oven for 30 minutes. Serve hot.

VEGETABLE SHEPHERD'S PIE   *Serves 2–3*

Make enough of the vegetable mixture for several helpings if possible, it's hardly worth cooking tiny amounts of pulses and you can freeze extra portions for later. The pie can be heated through in the oven if cooking from cold, or just crisped under a hot grill if the filling and potato topping are already hot.

Preparation and cooking time: 45 minutes
plus 45 mins. if using dried green
lentils
or plus 20 mins. if using dried red
Filling   lentils.
Lentil Bolognese Sauce – see page 58

Topping
3–4 potatoes (depending on size and appetite)
1 oz/25g butter
2 oz/50g Cheddar cheese – grated
Salt, pepper, shake of nutmeg
1–2 tomatoes

Prepare Lentil Bolognese Sauce (see page 58) but use a little less liquid (stir in only 1 cupful initially) so that you make a really good, thick sauce.

Prepare topping – peel and thickly slice (1"/2½cm) potatoes, and cook for about 10 minutes in gently boiling salted water until soft (do not overcook). Drain well and mash with a fork or masher, then beat with a wooden spoon until fluffy. Beat in half the butter, grated cheese, salt and pepper and a little grated nutmeg.

Pour vegetable mixture into a deep pie dish, casserole dish or individual dishes. Cover thickly with potato topping and fork down smoothly. Decorate top with thinly sliced tomatoes, dot with remaining butter and brown under a hot grill, if the filling and topping are still hot.

If cooking from cold (the pie can be prepared in advance and frozen or kept in the fridge until needed), heat through completely in a moderate oven 190°C/375°F/gas 5–6 for 15–20 minutes (shortest time for smallest dishes) until pie is hot and topping is lightly browned and crispy.

If you have freezer portions of vegetarian Bolognese Sauce in the freezer, it is very easy to defrost and cover them with the potato topping, to produce an "instant" Shepherd's Pie.

For a change or extra nourishment, add a well beaten egg to the potato topping, with or instead of the cheese; it makes a lovely fluffy top.

VEGETABLE GOULASH   *1 generous helping*

This recipe make a good, filling meal for one hungry person.

Preparation and cooking time: 45 minutes.

1 small onion
1 stick of celery
1 small carrot
1 courgette
1 very small chunk of white cabbage (enough to chop up into 3–4 tablespoonfuls)
1 medium potato
1 tblsp vegetable oil for frying
½ small (7 oz/230g) can tomatoes or 2 fresh tomatoes (washed or chopped)
2 tblsp cooked (see page 77) or canned red kidney beans (you can use up any left-over cooked beans)

(continued overleaf)

(Vegetable Goulash continued)

or 2 tblsp dried split red lentils
1 tsp tomato purée or tomato ketchup
¼ tsp vegetable extract
½ vegetable stock cube
¼ pt/142ml/1 cup water
1 tsp paprika pepper
Salt, pepper, ½ tsp dried mixed herbs
2 tsp cream, soured cream or yoghurt
Parsley for garnish

Peel and slice onion, wash and chop celery into 1″/2½cm lengths, peel and slice carrot (¼″/½cm rings), wash and thickly slice courgette (1″/2½cm lengths), wash and coarsely shred cabbage. Peel potato and cut into bite-sized chunks (not thin rings).

Heat oil in a medium-sized saucepan, fry onion and celery for 4–5 minutes over a medium heat until softened. Add carrot, courgette and cabbage and continue to cook for a further 5 minutes, stirring frequently.

Stir in canned or fresh tomatoes, cooked kidney beans or dried lentils, tomato purée or ketchup, vegetable extract, crumbled stock cube, water, paprika, seasoning and herbs.

Add potato chunks, bring to the boil, stirring occasionally, then reduce heat and leave to simmer with lid on, stirring occasionally (being careful not to break up the vegetable pieces) for 20 minutes, until lentils, potatoes and carrot are cooked (test with a knife) adding a little more liquid if necessary during cooking; there should be plenty of gravy.

Serve into a deep plate or bowl, spoon a little cream, yoghurt or soured cream over the top, and garnish with a few sprigs of scissor-snipped washed parsley.

Eat with hot granary bread or a chunk of French bread.

VEGETABLE AND WALNUT HOTPOT

Serves 2

This is best cooked in the oven, not simmered on top of the stove, as the vegetables absorb most of the stock, and would probably burn, even over a very low heat. It's easier to make enough for two, as an individual portion would tend to dry up too quickly.

Preparation and cooking time: 1 hour.

1 onion
1 stick of celery

Any mixture of the following:
>   1 carrot
>   1 tiny turnip or carrot-sized chunk of swede
>   1 small parsnip
>   1 small leek
>   Few sprigs of cauliflower
>   3–4 mushrooms
>   2 tblsp frozen or canned sweetcorn
>   2 tblsp frozen or canned peas

2 oz/50g/½ cup walnuts, or pecan nuts
1–2 potatoes (according to size and appetite)
1 tblsp vegetable oil
Salt, pepper
½ tsp mixed herbs
1 vegetable stock cube
¼ tsp vegetable extract
1 cup boiling water
2 oz/50g Cheddar or Edam cheese – grated

Heat oven – 180°C/350°F/gas 4–5.

Prepare vegetables: peel and slice onion, wash and slice celery, put into a saucepan or frying pan.

Peel and slice carrot, peel turnip, swede and parsnip thickly, and cut into ½″/2cm dice, trim and wash leek very thoroughly (slit down side and rinse well in cold, running water) and slice thickly, break cauli into small sprigs and wash well, wash and slice mushrooms, and mix all the vegetables together in a bowl with the sweetcorn and peas (no need to thaw) and nuts.

Peel and thickly slice potatoes (do not mix in with other vegetables).

Add oil to onion and celery, and cook over a moderate heat for 4–5 minutes until softened. Pour into a casserole dish, then put layers of the mixed vegetables into the dish, seasoning each layer with salt, pepper and herbs.

Dissolve stock cube and vegetable extract in the boiling water and pour over the vegetables. Cover vegetables with a thick lid of sliced potato. Sprinkle with grated cheese.

Bake in the hot oven for 35–40 minutes, until the stock is absorbed and the top is bubbly and golden (cover lightly with cooking foil if it gets too brown before the vegetables are cooked).

Serve hot, with crusty bread if you're extra hungry.

VEGETABLE CHILLI   *Serves 2–3*

Use the recipe for Lentil Bolognese (see page 58) adding chilli powder, tabasco sauce and cooked kidney beans to the basic recipe. It's very tasty and makes a good, hearty meal served with rice, jacket potatoes or chunks of new bread. Unless you have some left-over pre-cooked kidney beans, it's much easier to use canned kidney beans in this recipe.

Preparation and cooking time: 30 minutes
plus 45 minutes if using dried green
lentils
or plus 20 minutes if using dried red
lentils.

Lentil Bolognese Sauce
1–2 tsp chilli powder ⎫
Few drops of tabasco sauce ⎬   **according to taste**
⎭
2 cups pre-cooked or canned red kidney beans (remember that
dried kidney beans *must* be soaked then boiled hard for
the first 10 minutes of cooking time, see page 76).

Prepare Lentil Bolognese Sauce – see page 58 – adding the
chilli powder and tabasco sauce with the salt, pepper, sugar
and herbs, but do be cautious with the tabasco, a little goes a
long way! Stir in the cooked or canned kidney beans for the
last 10 minutes of cooking time.
    Serve hot, with a crunchy side salad to cool the palate!

SAVOURY VEGETABLE CRUMBLE

Serves 1

You can use fresh, new root vegetables or use up cooked
vegetables in this dish.

Preparation and cooking time: 45 minutes.

Topping
2 oz/50g/2 very heaped tblsp flour – wholemeal or white
1 oz/25g margarine or butter
1 oz/25g cheese – grated (optional)
1 oz/25g/1 tblsp chopped mixed nuts
1–2 tsp sesame or pumpkin seeds (optional)
Salt

Filling
1 onion
**4 oz/100g/1 full cup of any mixture of root vegetables, cooked
      or raw – 1 carrot, piece of swede, 1 parsnip etc.**
1 tblsp oil for frying
½ tsp flour or cornflour
½ cup/2½ fl oz/70ml boiling water
½ vegetable stock cube
Salt, pepper
¼ tsp curry powder or cayenne pepper (optional)
Dash of tabasco or Worcester sauce (optional)
1 tomato, thinly sliced, for decoration

Heat oven – 190°C/375°F/gas 5–6.

For the crumble topping: rub flour and margarine or butter
together with your fingertips until it looks like breadcrumbs.
Add cheese, nuts, seeds (if used) and salt. Mix together and
put aside.

For the filling: peel and slice onion, peel and thinly slice raw
vegetables or slice cooked vegetables thickly.

Heat oil in a saucepan over a medium heat and fry onion
gently for 3–4 minutes until softened. Add prepared
vegetables and continue to cook, stirring occasionally for
4–5 minutes.

Mix flour or cornflour in a cup with a tblsp cold water to
make a runny paste. Stir in the boiling water and crumble
stock cube, then stir the flour mixture into the vegetable
mixture and cook over a low heat until sauce thickens.
Reduce heat and simmer for 5–10 minutes until vegetables
are soft. Remove pan from heat. (If using cooked vegetables,
remove pan from heat when sauce has thickened.)

Pour vegetable mixture into an individual deep pie dish,
top with the crumble mixture and smooth over with a fork.

Decorate with sliced tomatoes, and bake in the hot oven for 15 minutes, until top is lightly browned.

This is good with new potatoes, green vegetables and gravy (see page 175).

Savoury vegetable crumble freezes well, it is easy to make double the quantity and is a useful quick meal to keep ready in the freezer.

MOUSSAKA
2 servings

Moussaka is a bit fiddly to make, but once you have prepared the three separate layers it's very quick and easy to assemble. This recipe is for 2 helpings; if you want an individual portion freeze one serving before baking, ready for defrosting and cooking in the future.

Preparation and cooking time: 45 minutes (plus 30 minutes to drain aubergine slices and make Bolognese Sauce).

1 large or 2 small aubergines
1 x "2 serving" quantity Bolognese sauce – see pages 164, 58, 59 (T.S.P., Lentil or Leek and Mushroom)
1 x ¼ pt/142ml/1 cup quantity Cheese Sauce – see page 176
1–2 tblsp vegetable oil for frying
1–2 tblsp Parmesan cheese, grated for topping (optional)

Wash and slice aubergines (¼"/½cm), put in layers in a colander, sprinkle with salt and leave to drain for 30 minutes (see page 131).

Prepare chosen Bolognese Sauce – see pages 164, 58, 59.
Make Cheese Sauce – see page 59.
Rinse aubergine slices and dry on kitchen paper.
Heat oven – 200°C/400°F/gas 6–7.

Heat oil in a frying pan over a moderate heat and fry aubergine slices for a few minutes on each side until lightly coloured. Drain on more kitchen paper. Add a little more oil to the pan and fry any remaining aubergines.

Use 2 individual dishes (foil ones are useful) or a larger deep flan-type dish. Starting with Bolognese, put alternate layers of Bolognese sauce and aubergine slices in the dish or dishes, ending with aubergines. Pour the cheese sauce over the top, and sprinkle with the Parmesan cheese (if used).

Freeze any extra portions now, ready to defrost later when needed.

Bake in the hot oven for 20 minutes – individual dishes
                    30 minutes – larger dish
until top is a lovely golden brown. Serve with wholemeal bread and crunchy green salad.

PILAFF WITH BULGAR WHEAT   *1 portion*

Try Bulgar (or Burghul or Cracked) Wheat Pilaff as it is a nourishing tasty change from rice. Serve plain pilaff as an accompaniment to other dishes, or add some extras and turn it into a main meal, served with a crisp green salad.

Preparation and cooking time: 30 minutes.

½ small onion
1 clove of fresh garlic or ¼ tsp crushed garlic
1 tblsp vegetable oil
2 oz/50g/½ cup bulgar, burghul or cracked wheat
½ vegetable stock cube
1 cup/¼ pt/142ml boiling water
1 oz/25g butter

Peel and finely chop onion and fresh garlic. Heat oil in a saucepan over a moderate heat and fry onion and garlic for 4–5 minutes, until just softened but not brown. Add bulgar wheat and continue to fry gently for a further 3–4 minutes. Dissolve stock cube in the boiling water and add to the pan, stir well and cover pan and simmer gently for 8–10 minutes, until the liquid is absorbed and the bulgar is soft – add a little more water if it gets too dry before the wheat is cooked.

Remove from the heat, stir in the butter, cover again with a tightly fitting lid and leave for 5–10 minutes, either on a turned-off hot plate or on the lowest possible heat, to allow the bulgar to swell up, absorb the flavours and become light and fluffy.

Serve instead of boiled rice.

Variations

WALNUT AND TOMATO PILAFF
Stir in 1–2 washed, chopped tomatoes, fresh or canned, with the stock and cook with the bulgar wheat. Then add 1 oz/25g/1 tblsp chopped walnuts with the butter, stir well and leave bulgar to fluff up in the tightly covered pan.

PINE KERNEL PILAFF
Stir 1 tblsp pine kernels into the cooked bulgar wheat with the butter. Cover with the lid and leave to fluff up as before.

SWEET PEPPER AND HERB PILAFF
Wash and finely chop ½ small green pepper. Add with the bulgar wheat to the onion in the saucepan and fry gently for 3–4 minutes, then add stock and cook as in basic recipe. When bulgar wheat is cooked, stir in butter and a few sprigs of washed, scissor-snipped parsley, chives or mint. Cover with a tightly fitting lid and leave to fluff up as before.

CHINESE STIR FRY   *Serves 1*

Stir fry means exactly what it says: the vegetables are cut into
small pieces or shredded, then fried quickly for a few
minutes, stirred all the time until cooked, then seasoned and
served immediately.

Preparation and cooking time: 15 minutes.

2–3 spring onions or 1 small onion
1 medium-size carrot
2 oz/50g/1 large cup full shredded Chinese leaves
3 oz/75g bean sprouts
1 tblsp vegetable oil
1–2 tblsp cashew nuts or pine nut kernels (optional)
1–2 tsp soy sauce
Pinch of sugar, salt, black pepper

Wash spring onions, cut off roots and any unappetising-
looking green parts and chop into rings, or peel and slice
onion. Peel carrot and cut into matchsticks. Wash shredded
Chinese leaves. Wash and drain bean sprouts. The
vegetables can all be prepared in advance if necessary.

Heat oil in a frying pan or wok. Add all the vegetables and
stir fry briskly for 1–2 minutes, until hot and crispy. Add
nuts, soy sauce and sugar, season to taste with salt and black
pepper.

Mix well and serve immediately.

CURRY   *Serves 1 or 2*
                           (according to appetite)

Make a mild or hot curry sauce according to taste. It can

then be served as a vegetable curry, using either fresh, raw vegetables, frozen vegetables (there are special packs sold for stews and casseroles) or you can use up left-over cooked vegetables. The sauce can also be used with hard-boiled eggs for a tasty egg curry, or if you're really hungry, have a vegetable curry with eggs.

Preparation and cooking time: 45 minutes.

Curry Sauce
1 small onion
1 small apple – cooking or eating
1 tsp lemon juice
1 tblsp vegetable oil for frying
**1–2 tsp curry powder – either mild or hot, according to
     preference**
½ vegetable stock cube
1 cup/¼ pt/142ml boiling water
1–2 tomatoes – quartered
1 tsp brown sugar
1 tsp sweet pickle or chutney
1 tsp sultanas

Peel and slice onion. Peel and chop apple and toss it in lemon juice. Heat oil in saucepan over a moderate heat and fry onion for 3–4 minutes stirring occasionally, until softened. Add chopped apple, stir in curry powder and continue to cook gently for a further 2–3 minutes. Mix crumbled stock cube in boiling water, and stir into onion mixture, with tomato pieces, brown sugar, pickle or chutney and washed, drained sultanas. Bring to the boil, then reduce heat and simmer gently with the lid on, for about 10 minutes stirring occasionally, to make a good, thick sauce:

Vegetable Curry

8 oz/225g/2 full cups mixed vegetables – carrots, cauliflower, celery, cooked beans, peppers, potatoes, swede, turnip etc. Keep raw and cooked vegetables separate at this stage, if using both.

Prepare fresh vegetables, if used, cut into largish bite-sized pieces, and cook in boiling salted water for 5–10 minutes until tender but still *al dente*. Drain well. (You can cook the different kinds of veg together in the same pan.) Slice any left-over cooked vegetables. Cook frozen vegetables following instructions on the packets.

Gently stir all the vegetables into the curry sauce, and simmer for a further 5–10 minutes, until the vegetables are heated right through and completely cooked.

Serve curry on a bed of rice, with poppadums and side dishes

Egg Curry

Hard boil 1 or 2 eggs, by simmering in salted water for 10 minutes, then plunge them into cold water and peel off the shells.

Cook and drain rice, and form into a hollow ring on a serving dish.

Slice eggs in half and place in centre of rice ring. Cover with curry sauce, and serve with poppadums and side dishes.

Poppadums

Great fun to cook – packets of poppadums are on sale at most supermarkets. Heat 3–4 tblsp cooking oil (enough to cover base of pan) in a frying pan over a medium heat. When oil is hot, float a poppadum on top and it will puff up immediately, only taking a few moments to cook. Remove it carefully and drain on kitchen paper, while cooking next poppadum. Do not let the fat get too hot, or it will get smoky and burn.

Poppadums are most spectacular, cooked in the microwave oven, and are less greasy as they are cooked without fat. Just place 1 or 2 poppadums on a sheet of kitchen paper in the microwave, and cook on high for a few seconds. You can watch the flat cakes rise to become puffed and crispy before your very eyes!

Serving suggestions for side dishes

Salted nuts
Chopped green or red peppers
Chopped tomatoes
Sliced bananas ⎤ Sprinkled with lemon juice
Chopped apple ⎦ to stop browning
Chopped cucumber
Sliced onion
Chopped hard-boiled egg
Washed, drained sultanas
Desiccated coconut
Plain yoghurt, on its own, or mixed with a little lemon juice and chopped cucumber.

PLOUGHMAN'S PASTIES   *2 pasties*

A tasty alternative to traditional Cornish pasties, but the two recipes could easily be prepared together. You can of course, use white shortcrust pastry, (home-made or frozen) if you prefer.

Preparation and cooking time: 55–60 minutes.

**8 oz/200g quantity wholemeal shortcrust pastry (use
  4 oz/100g flour, 2 oz/50g fat) see page 70**
**4 oz/100g mixed root vegetables – onion, carrot, swede, turnip,
  potato (use any mixture but include some onion)**
2 oz/50g cheese – Cheddar or Edam
1 tsp vegetable oil
$\frac{1}{2}$ tsp mixed herbs
Few sprigs of fresh parsley and/or chives – if available
Salt, pepper
Little milk for brushing

Heat oven – 200°C/400°F/gas 6–7.

Make pastry (see page 70) and leave in fridge while preparing filling.

Peel and chop or finely dice ($\frac{1}{4}$″/$\frac{1}{2}$cm) chosen root vegetables and put into a bowl. Grate cheese, and mix into vegetables with the vegetable oil, mixed herbs, washed scissor-snipped parsley and chives and season well with salt and pepper.

Sprinkle a little flour onto a clean work surface, and roll out pastry (about $\frac{1}{4}$″/$\frac{1}{2}$cm thick) and cut out 2 rounds, approximately 7″/18cm wide (cut round a plate, basin or saucepan lid). Divide the filling between the two pasties, brush edges of pastry with milk and fold over to form a pasty shape (if you put the filling on one half of the pastry it will be easier to fold it over). Pinch edges together very firmly, and either leave in a flat, semi-circular shape or stand on edge with the seam running along the top. Place on a baking sheet. Brush with milk and carefully prick sides or top with tip of a vegetable knife to let the steam escape. Bake in the hot oven for 15 minutes, then reduce heat to 170°C/325°F/gas 3–4 for a further 15–20 minutes to cook the filling completely.

Serve pasties hot or cold, either on their own or with salad or vegetables.

EGG AND CHEESE DISHES

VEGETARIAN SCOTCH EGGS

2 eggs

Makes a delicious change in a lunch box or for a picnic, or served at home hot or cold, with new or jacket potatoes, vegetables or salad for a main meal.

Preparation and cooking time: 30 minutes plus at least 30 minutes standing time if possible.

2 eggs
1 tblsp wholemeal or white flour
1 quantity of vege sausage – see page 153

Coating
Little beaten egg
2–3 tblsp dried breadcrumbs
Vegetable oil for frying – you can shallow fry or use deep fat
    frying

Hard boil eggs (simmer in boiling, salted water for 10 minutes, drain and plunge eggs into cold water). Peel off egg shell, rinse in cold water to remove any clinging shell, and dry on kitchen paper. Coat each egg in a little flour.

Prepare vege sausage (see page 153) and divide into two equal pieces and flatten each piece to a 5″/13cm circle. Place a flour-coated egg on each piece and carefully pull the sausage mixture round each egg until the egg is completely covered. Seal the joints thoroughly and smoothly, and roll egg gently to make a good round shape. Leave eggs to stand in a cool place for at least 30 minutes if possible, so that the vege sausage mixture becomes firm and less likely to crumble during cooking.

Deep Frying: Pour beaten egg into a soup bowl and sprinkle dried breadcrumbs into another bowl. Dip each Scotch egg into the beaten egg and then coat thoroughly with the dried breadcrumbs. Heat oil in the deep fat pan to 180°C/350°F/gas 4–5 (not too hot or the eggs will burn on the outside before the inside is cooked), and fry eggs in the frying basket for 4–5 minutes until golden brown. Drain well on kitchen paper and serve hot or cold.

Shallow Frying: Coat in beaten egg and dried breadcrumbs or not as you wish, according to taste. Heat 3–4 tsp vegetable oil in a frying pan over a moderate heat and fry eggs gently for 6–8 minutes, turning frequently until browned evenly on all sides. Drain well on kitchen paper and serve hot or cold.

EGGY VEGETABLE BAKE   *1 generous helping*

A tasty filling supper dish, quick and easy to prepare and you can use up the odds and ends of vegetables which seem to accumulate in the fridge or vegetable drawer, especially after a weekend of family meals.

Preparation and cooking time: 1 hour 15 minutes.

2–3 potatoes (according to size and appetite)
1 carrot
2–3 sprigs of cauliflower
2–3 mushrooms
1 tblsp sliced green beans and/or peas (cooked, fresh or frozen)
1 tblsp sweetcorn (cooked, canned or frozen)
2 oz/50g cheese
1 egg
½ cup/2½ fl oz /70ml milk
Salt, pepper
Knob of butter

Heat oven – 180°C/350°F/gas 4–5.

Grease a small casserole or deep oven-proof dish well.

Wash, peel and slice the vegetables, do not cut them too small (bite-sized chunks) and mix them together in a bowl. Grate cheese.

Put vegetable mixture in layers in the buttered dish, scattering cheese between each layer. Beat egg, add milk, salt and pepper, mix well and pour over vegetable mixture. Dot with butter, cover lightly with cooking foil and bake in a moderate oven for 45 minutes, until the egg is set and the top is golden brown – remove foil for last 20 minutes of cooking time.

EGGS FLORENTINE   *Serves 1 or 2*

This dish can be made from fresh or frozen spinach or other

vegetables which you may have fresh or left-over from being cooked previously – celery, courgettes or mashed swede and carrot. It makes a starter or light meal and is a good dish for slimmers.

Preparation and cooking time: 30 minutes.

½ small packet (4 oz/100g) frozen spinach
or 8 oz/225g fresh spinach
¼ pt/142ml/1 cup cheese sauce – see page 176 and 1 extra
    tablespoon of grated cheese
or 2 oz/50g Cheddar or Edam cheese, grated
Knob of butter
Squeeze of lemon juice
2 eggs

Cook frozen spinach as directed on the packet or wash well, chop and cook fresh spinach (in a large pan with no extra water) over a medium heat for 7–10 minutes until soft. Alternatively cook other types of vegetables or reheat cooked vegetables in a greased, oven-proof dish in a moderate oven (190°C/375°F/gas 5–6) for 10 minutes or heat in a microwave according to oven instructions.

Make cheese sauce if used – see page 176 (reserve the extra cheese).

Drain spinach very well, pressing out the water to get spinach as dry as possible. Stir in knob of butter and a squeeze of lemon juice. Put into a warm oven-proof serving dish, and keep warm.

Poach eggs in a clean frying pan in 1″/2½cm simmering water (crack eggs one at a time into a cup and slide them into the simmering water and cook gently for about 3 minutes until egg is set) or cook in a poacher according to directions. Carefully remove cooked eggs with a slotted spoon or fish slice, being careful not to break the yolks underneath, and put them on top of the spinach or hot vegetables.

Heat grill.

Coat eggs with cheese sauce and sprinkle reserved cheese on top, or cover poached eggs with grated cheese. Brown for a few minutes under a hot grill until the cheese topping is crisp and bubbling.

CHEESY LENTIL WEDGES   *4 slices*

Serve cold with salad, as a nice change from sandwiches in a lunch box, or hot as a main meal, when they are good with home-made tomato sauce and vegetables.

Preparation and cooking time: 55–60 minutes.

1 small onion
1 clove of garlic or ¼ tsp garlic granules (optional)
2 tsp vegetable oil
4 oz/100g/1 generous cup split red lentils
½ pt/284ml/2 cups water
1 bay leaf
2 oz/50g Cheddar or Edam cheese
1 tblsp grated Parmesan cheese
¼ tsp chilli powder – optional
Few sprigs of fresh parsley
Salt, pepper
1–2 tomatoes

Peel and finely chop onion and fresh garlic. Heat oil in a saucepan over a moderate heat and fry onion and garlic gently for 3–4 minutes until just softened but not browned. Rinse lentils in a sieve and add to onion with the water and bay leaf, stir well and bring to the boil, then reduce heat and simmer for 20–25 minutes until the water is absorbed and the lentils are tender (watch pan for last few minutes to make sure the lentils do not boil dry and burn).

Heat oven – 200°C/400°F/gas 6–7. Grease a 6″/15cm sandwich tin. Remove lentils from heat and discard bay leaf. Grate Cheddar or Edam cheese, reserve 2 tblsp, and beat the rest into the lentil mixture with the Parmesan cheese, chilli powder, washed scissor-snipped parsley, salt and pepper. Put mixture into well-greased tin and spread evenly. Sprinkle reserved cheese over the top and decorate with tomato slices.

Bake in the hot oven for 15–20 minutes until golden brown and crispy. Serve hot or cold.

CHEDDAR CHICK PEAS   *2 helpings*

You need such small amounts of these ingredients that it is easier to make enough for 2 servings, freezing one helping if necessary. It is easier to use canned chick peas unless you have some left-over cooked ones from a previous recipe, although I have given the amount of dried chick peas in case you prefer to cook them specially.

Preparation and cooking time: 30 minutes (plus soaking time and 45 minutes cooking time if using dried chick peas).

1 small (7 oz/230g) can chick peas (keep the liquid in the can)
or
4 oz/100g dried chick peas, soaked and cooked (see page 76).
     Save the cooking water.
1 small onion

1 small (7 oz/230g) can tomatoes or 3–4 fresh tomatoes,
    washed
4 oz/100g fresh spinach
or
2 oz/50g/1 cup defrosted frozen spinach
1 tblsp vegetable oil and a little butter for frying
1 tsp mixed dried herbs
½ tsp paprika pepper
2 oz/50g Cheddar cheese – grated
Salt, pepper
2–3 tblsp natural yoghurt

Strain canned or cooked chick peas, saving a cup of the
liquid. Blend half the chick peas in a liquidiser with 3–4 tblsp
of liquid, or mash the peas with a fork in a small basin adding
3–4 tblsp of liquid gradually.

Peel and chop onion, chop tomatoes, wash fresh spinach
very well under running water, shake dry and very finely
shred it.

Heat oil and butter in a medium saucepan, fry onion over a
moderate heat for 3–4 minutes until soft. Add the whole
chick peas and cook for a further 2–3 minutes, stirring all the
time.

Stir in fresh or defrosted spinach, chopped tomatoes,
blended or mashed chick peas, herbs and seasoning and
continue to simmer for 4–5 minutes stirring occasionally.
Remove from heat, mix in grated cheese and serve topped
with yoghurt and a shake of paprika pepper.

If one helping is to be frozen, it is best frozen before the
addition of the grated cheese. When this frozen portion is
eventually needed, defrost it thoroughly. Heat through in a
small saucepan over a moderate heat, stirring gently,
allowing it to simmer for 3–4 minutes. Stir in the grated
cheese and serve topped with yoghurt and paprika as above.

CHEESY AUBERGINE LAYER   *Serves 1*

I try and keep some home-made tomato sauce in individual portions in the freezer, ready to defrost and use quickly when needed.

Preparation and cooking time: 50 minutes (or 30 minutes if the tomato sauce is already cooked).

See note at end of recipe about draining aubergines for 30–60 minutes before cooking.

¼ pt/142ml/1 cup tomato sauce – see page 178
1 medium-size aubergine
1 tblsp vegetable oil for frying
2 oz/50g Mozzarella, Cheddar or Edam cheese, cut into thin
    slices
1 tblsp grated Parmesan cheese

Heat oven – 200°C/400°F/gas 6–7.

Grease a deep, individual dish (Pyrex or foil type). Make tomato sauce, or leave a portion to defrost.

Wash and slice aubergine into ¼"/½cm slices. Drain with salt, if you wish. See note. Dry slices with kitchen paper.

Heat oil in frying pan and fry aubergine slices for a few minutes over a moderate heat, turning once, until both sides are slightly coloured. Drain on kitchen paper. Add more oil to pan and fry any remaining aubergine slices.

Put a layer of tomato sauce into the greased dish, cover with a layer of fried aubergine slices, more tomato sauce and then a layer of cheese slices. Repeat layers until the ingredients are used up, finishing with a cheese layer.

Sprinkle top with grated Parmesan cheese.

Bake in the hot oven for 15 minutes until the top is a crispy

golden brown.
  Serve hot with jacket potato or bread rolls.

Note: Aubergines can taste bitter, although this taste is masked by the cheese in this recipe. However, if you have time slice the aubergines and put the slices in layers in a colander to drain, sprinkling each layer with salt. Stand colander on a plate to catch the drips, and cover aubergines with a plate to press them down. Leave to drain for 30–60 minutes. Rinse and dry aubergine slices with kitchen paper. They are now ready for frying.

COURGETTES WITH CHEESE SAVOURY
1 generous helping or 2 starters

A tasty lunch or supper dish, delicious served with small mint-flavoured new potatoes or warm brown rolls. It also makes a good starter, served in individual ramekin dishes. Use courgettes or marrow as available.

Preparation and cooking time: 30–35 minutes.

½ lb/200g/1–2 courgettes or piece of marrow
Salt, pepper
1 small onion
2 tsp vegetable oil
1 egg
2 oz/50g Cheddar, Edam or Gruyère cheese
Few sprigs of fresh parsley, if possible
1–2 tsp grated Parmesan cheese

Heat oven – 190°C/375°F/gas 5–6.
  Grease an individual dish or 2 ramekin dishes.

Top and tail, wash and cut courgettes into 1"/2½cm slices, or peel marrow and cut into bite-sized chunks. Simmer gently in a very little boiling salted water for 2–3 minutes, until just tender – don't use too much water or all the flavour will boil away; about ½–1 cupful/2½–5 fl oz/70–142ml should be plenty. Drain well, as the slices tend to be a bit watery (you can get them really dry by shaking them in the pan over a very low heat for a moment or two). Put into the greased dish or ramekins.

Peel and finely slice onion, warm oil in a pan over a moderate heat and fry onion for 3–4 minutes until softened but not browned. Pour onion over courgettes in dish.

Beat egg in a small basin. Grate Cheddar, Edam or Gruyère cheese and add to the beaten egg with the salt, pepper and washed scissor-snipped parsley, and pour mixture over the vegetables. Sprinkle top with grated Parmesan and bake in the moderate oven for 10–15 minutes until the egg is set.

Serve at once.

POSH NOSH

Dishes for entertaining and impressing your friends, or just to enjoy with all the family. These recipes may be helpful if you are entertaining a vegetarian friend too.

The ingredients in this section may be a little more expensive than most of the recipes in the book, but they are certainly not outrageous.

I'm sure lots of these recipes will be enjoyed by the non-converted if you have a "mixed" dinner party (remember non-vegetarians can eat vegetarian food, but vegetarians won't eat meat). Try serving little mushroom feuilletés as a dinner party starter or the Bean and Vegetable Gougère or the lovely Aubergine Imam Bayildi and I don't think you'll have many complaints.

MUSHROOM STROGANOFF   *Serves 1*

Very quick and easy to prepare (and similar but much

cheaper than the non-vegetarian Beef Stroganoff!). Serve with plain brown rice.

Preparation and cooking time: 20 minutes.

1 small onion
1 clove of garlic or $\frac{1}{4}$ tsp minced garlic
1 stick of celery
4 oz/100g mushrooms
Few strips of green pepper
$\frac{1}{2}$ oz/12g butter, and a little oil for frying
2 oz/50g/$\frac{1}{2}$ cup cashew nuts
2 tblsp cream, soured cream or yoghurt
Salt, pepper
Few sprigs of parsley or chives

Peel and slice onion and fresh garlic, wash and chop celery, wash and slice mushrooms, wash and chop pepper strips.

Melt butter and oil in frying pan over a medium heat, and fry onion, garlic and celery for 4–5 minutes until soft but not brown. Add a little more oil and butter, if necessary, then add mushrooms and pepper and stir gently over a medium heat for a further 4–5 minutes.

Stir in nuts and heat thoroughly.

Remove from heat, stir in cream, soured cream or yoghurt, and then reheat very carefully; but do not allow the sauce to boil (or it may curdle).

Serve on a bed of cooked rice, sprinkled with washed, scissor-snipped parsley or chives. It is also delicious with new potatoes and a green vegetable, or a crunchy side salad.

MUSHROOM AND PARMESAN ROULADE
Serves 2–3 (depending on appetite)

You will need a whisk or mixer for this recipe. When giving a

posh dinner party make double the quantity in the larger tin.
The filling can be made in advance and kept in the fridge, but
the roulade is best prepared, baked and eaten immediately.
The recipe below gives 2 very generous portions.

Preparation and cooking time: 45 minutes.

Filling
1 small onion
4 oz/100g mushrooms
1 tblsp vegetable oil
½ cup white wine, cider or vegetable stock (use ½ crumbled
      stock cube in boiling water)
Salt, pepper
1–2 tblsp double cream, soured cream or yoghurt
1 tblsp grated Parmesan cheese
Handful of parsley or chives or other fresh green herbs to taste

Roulade
3 eggs
Salt, pepper
½ tsp mustard
4 oz/100g Cheddar or Edam cheese, grated

2 sheets greaseproof or silicone non-stick paper.

Heat oven – 200°C/400°F/gas 6–7.
    Grease a 7 x 11″/18 x 28cm Swiss roll tin, then line the base
and sides with greaseproof or silicone paper (put paper in tin
and press into shape, then snip corners so that paper fits
tightly, coming 2″/5cm above sides of tin). If making a
double quantity roulade, use a 9 x 13″/23 x 33cm tin.
    For the filling: Peel and chop onion, wash and slice

mushrooms. Heat oil in a small saucepan for 4–5 minutes. Add mushrooms and continue to cook for a further 2–3 minutes, then stir in wine, cider or stock. Season well with salt and pepper. Simmer with lid on for 2–3 minutes to cook vegetables, then remove lid and boil rapidly for a few minutes to reduce the liquid to 1–2 tblsp. Remove from heat, stir in cream or yoghurt and leave in the fridge until needed.

For the roulade: Separate the eggs, putting yolks into a small basin and whites into a large bowl. Whisk egg yolks with salt, pepper and mustard until light yellow and quite thick. Using a metal spoon carefully fold in cheese. (Do not stir the cheese in too vigorously, but cut it into the mixture or the air bubbles will be broken and roulade will not rise. Always use a metal spoon or knife when folding in ingredients.)

Wash whisk or mixer beaters, then whip egg whites until well risen, stiff and dry (you can test this by turning the bowl upside down, this mixture *should* stay in the bowl, but it's rather a risky procedure!). Very gently fold in 1 tblsp of the stiff whites into the yolk mixture to make it softer, then fold the rest of the yolk mixture into the whites, until evenly mixed.

Pour into prepared tin, smoothing lightly with a knife, but be careful not to break the air bubbles.

Bake in the hot oven for 8–10 minutes – small tin
10–12 minutes – large tin.

Remove roulade from oven when well risen, firm and golden brown. Leave oven on. Put a sheet of greaseproof or silicone paper on table, sprinkle generously with the Parmesan cheese, then tip roulade onto the paper.

Reheat mushroom mixture over a low heat, but do not allow it to boil. Then spoon it evenly over the roulade. Scissor-snip washed herbs over filling and roll roulade up carefully, like a Swiss roll.

Using a fish slice, put it onto a warm, oven-proof plate and put into the oven for 3–4 minutes to reheat right through.

This is delicious served with new potatoes and fresh green vegetables for a posh dinner, or with crusty bread rolls and a side salad for supper.

MUSHROOM FEUILLETÉ   *Serves 2*

This is so delicious it is far too nice to eat alone and I'm sure any non-vegetarians in the family will want to try it. The sauce is very rich, so it's a more filling dish than it may appear from the recipe. It's very impressive served with new potatoes, French beans and a green salad. Tiny feuilletés would make a good starter, just cut smaller pastry circles.

Preparation and cooking time: 30 minutes plus defrosting time for pastry.

⅓ 13 oz/370g packet frozen puff pastry – defrosted

Filling
6 oz/175g button mushrooms
4 oz/100g champignons (dark-coloured mushrooms)
1 clove of garlic or ¼ tsp ground garlic
½ oz/15g butter or marg
1 tblsp vegetable oil for frying
½ cup soured cream or yoghurt ⎫ Any mixture: approx.
½ cup double cream   ⎬ ¼ pt/142ml/1 cup
Salt, pepper   ⎭ altogether
Parsley and/or watercress for garnish

Heat oven – 210°C/425°F/gas 7–8.

Roll out pastry into a strip $\frac{1}{4}''$/$\frac{1}{2}$cm thick, or slightly thicker. Cut out 2 x 3"/7cm circles, using a pastry cutter or cut round a cup, and 2 x 2"/5cm circles, using a smaller pastry cutter or cut round a small glass. Put circles on a baking sheet (no need to grease) and bake in the hot oven for 10 minutes, until risen and golden. Put onto a cooling tray or grill rack, to keep them crisp.

For the filling: Wash and slice mushrooms, peel and chop fresh garlic. Heat butter and oil in a saucepan, add all the mushrooms and garlic, and fry over a low heat for about 5 minutes, stirring gently with a wooden spoon until mushrooms are cooked. Remove mushrooms into a dish or basin, using a slotted spoon. There will be a lot of juice left in the pan. Boil this rapidly for a few minutes, until it is reduced to about 1 tblsp. Put mushrooms back into pan with the reduced juices, stir in cream, soured cream or yoghurt and heat through gently; try not to let sauce boil or it may curdle.

Season with salt and pepper.

Reheat pastry circles in oven for a few minutes if they've gone cold. Put a large circle on each plate, spoon over the mushrooms and sauce and top with a small pastry circle.

Wash parsley and watercress, and scissor-snip a little parsley over the sauce. Garnish with watercress, and serve hot with vegetables.

MAHSHAR STIR FRY   *Serves 2*

If you have a guest to dinner, the vegetables can be cooked and the sauce mixed (but not cooked) in advance, just leaving you to add the cooked rice and nuts, heat the meal through and finish the sauce while the noodles are boiling. Serve with ribbon noodles, or a crunchy green salad and tiny new potatoes.

Preparation and cooking time: 30 minutes.

2 onions
4 oz/100g mushrooms
¼ cucumber
2 eating apples
½ red pepper
½ green pepper
½ cup cooked rice (use up left-over rice if you have it, otherwise
    cook 2 tblsp dry rice)
1 tblsp oil and a little butter for frying
2 oz/50g/½ cup cashew nuts
Few sprigs of parsley

Sweet and Sour Sauce
2 tsp cornflour
1 tblsp sugar
1 tsp soy sauce
2 tblsp vinegar
½ vegetable stock cube
½ cup boiling water

Peel and slice onions. Wash and slice mushrooms. Wash and
dice cucumber (½″/1cm). Peel and slice apples. Wash, core
and chop peppers. Cook rice if using dry rice (cooking in
boiling, salted water for 10 minutes, drain well).

Heat oil and butter in frying pan or wok over a moderate
heat and fry onion for 3–4 minutes until softened but not
brown. Add mushrooms, cucumber, apples and peppers and
continue to fry for a further 8–10 minutes, stirring gently
until the vegetables are cooked but not mushy (if preparing
vegetables in advance, cool and put in fridge until required).

Add cooked rice and cashew nuts and continue stir frying
until heated right through.

Tip into a warm serving dish or serve in the wok, and pour
sweet and sour sauce over mixture. Sprinkle with washed,
scissor-snipped parsley and serve.

Sweet and Sour Sauce
Put cornflour and sugar into a small saucepan and mix to a smooth paste with soy sauce and vinegar. Dissolve stock cube in half cup of boiling water and stir stock into mixture. Bring to the boil over a moderate heat, stirring all the time, and continue to simmer for 1–2 minutes, until sauce thickens and becomes transparent.

BEAN AND VEGETABLE GOUGÈRE

Serves 2–3

This is one of our favourite vegetarian recipes, and one that the non-vegetarians in our family will eat quite happily, without the usual quips about "have you forgotten the meat today?". It's a bit fiddly to make, but the filling can be prepared in advance and kept in the fridge until needed. It's far too nice to make in single portion size, so this recipe feeds two or three people.

Preparation and cooking time: filling – 30 minutes
choux pastry – 15 minutes.
gougère – 45 minutes in the oven.

Filling
2 oz/50g/2 heaped tblsp dried aduki beans, soaked then fast
    boiled for 10 minutes and cooked for ¾ hour (see page
    76)
1 small onion
1 stick of celery
1"/2cm chunk of cucumber

1 small (7 oz/230g) can tomatoes or 8 oz/200g fresh tomatoes
    (3–4 tomatoes)
1 tblsp vegetable oil for frying
1 tsp brown (or white) sugar
Pinch of chilli powder
2 tsp tomato purée or ketchup
½ tsp whole grain mustard or any mild mustard
2 tsp vinegar

Prepare and cook the aduki beans. These must be cooked properly as otherwise they are poisonous.

Peel and chop onion finely. Wash and chop celery. Wash cucumber and cut into tiny cubes. Chop tomatoes.

Put oil in a saucepan and fry onion and celery gently for 4–5 minutes until soft but not browned.

Mix sugar, chilli, tomato purée or ketchup and mustard with the vinegar, in a small basin or cup to make a runny paste. Add cucumber and tomatoes to onion and heat gently, stirring in the spices from the basin. Add the cooked aduki beans, stir well and simmer for about 15 minutes until the sauce has thickened (use a very low heat or the mixture may burn at the bottom), stirring occasionally.

The filling is now ready to use, or it may be kept in the fridge in a covered basin for use later in the day.

Choux Pastry Case
2 oz/50g marg (hard type) or butter
¼ pt/142ml/1 cup water
2 eggs
2½ oz/65g/3 very heaped tblsp plain white flour
or
2 heaped tblsp wholemeal plain flour with 1 very heaped tblsp
    self-raising white flour

Heat oven – 210°C/425°F/gas 7–8.

Grease well a flan dish or sandwich cake tin (8″/20cm size). The gougère is served in the dish, so a pretty one is nice!

Put marg or butter and water in a saucepan and melt fat slowly, bringing gradually to the boil.

Beat eggs well with a whisk or a fork in a basin; measure flour into another basin or small dish.

When fat and water is boiling, remove from heat and add flour immediately, all at once, beating hard with a wooden spoon to form a lump of dough.

Gradually beat in the eggs, a little at a time; beat very well with each addition. It will be very soft like a cake mixture.

Spoon the choux pastry round the sides (so that the egg-shaped spoonfuls of dough touch each other) to form a hollow ring shape and put a thin layer over the base of the well-greased dish.

Pour the filling into the flan, it will be quite full but the pastry will rise round the filling as it cooks.

Bake: 210°C/425°F/gas 7–8 for 25 minutes
        then lower heat to
        190°C/375°F/gas 5–6 for a further 15–20 minutes
until pastry is well risen, crisp and golden.

This is good with Creole salad and French bread or a jacket potato if you're very hungry.

VEGETABLE PANCAKES   *2 generous helpings*

The pancakes can be made in advance and kept in the fridge or freezer, filled or unfilled; then, covered in foil, heated through thoroughly in a warm oven.

Preparation and cooking time: 45–50 minutes.

Pancake Batter
4 tblsp/4 oz/100g plain flour
Pinch of salt
1 egg
½ pt/2 cups/284ml milk
Oil for frying

Filling
1 small onion
1 clove of garlic or ¼ tsp minced garlic
Tiny piece of fresh root ginger (about 1 tsp when chopped)
**   (optional) ·**
1 small carrot
6 oz/150g mushrooms
4 oz/100g beansprouts
1 tblsp vegetable oil for frying
2 tblsp cashew nuts
1 tblsp soy sauce
Salt, pepper
½ pt/284ml home-made tomato sauce (optional)

Make 6–8 pancakes (see page 30) and keep warm in a stack in a warm oven – 100°C/200°F/gas 1–2, while you make the filling.

For the filling: Peel and slice onion, peel and chop fresh garlic and root ginger if used. Peel carrot and cut into little matchsticks, wash and thinly slice mushrooms. Rinse beansprouts in cold water in a sieve and drain well. Heat 1 tblsp oil in a frying pan or wok over a moderate heat and fry onion, garlic, carrot and ginger for 2–3 minutes until slightly softened but still crunchy. Add mushrooms, and cook for a further 1–2 minutes. Add cashew nuts and beansprouts and season to taste with soy sauce, salt and pepper.

Increase oven temperature to – 180°C/350°F/gas 4–5.

Lay pancakes on a clean work surface and divide mixture between them. Roll pancakes up carefully or fold into quarters and carefully place them in a serving dish. Pour over tomato sauce if used, although the pancakes are tasty on their own. Cover dish lightly with foil and heat through in the hot oven for 8–10 minutes.

Serve with a crispy salad or green vegetables, new potatoes or bread rolls.

IMAM BAYILDI (STUFFED AUBERGINE)

Serves 1

A typical Middle Eastern vegetable dish, using aubergine (or egg plant) which is a great favourite there. Legend says this dish, which means "the Imam fainted", was so named when the Imam (Turkish holy man) fainted with pleasure on tasting it. A more cynical story says the Imam fainted when told the cost of the dish he had eaten. These days it's not quite so expensive to make!

Preparation and cooking time: 1 hour (plus about 1 hour to drain aubergine).

1 medium-sized aubergine

For each aubergine allow:
½ small onion
1 clove of garlic or ¼ tsp powdered garlic
1 tomato – fresh or canned
3 tblsp olive oil
Few sprigs of parsley
2 tsp lemon juice
Pinch of sugar
Salt, pepper

The aubergine should be salted and drained to get rid of the bitter-tasting juices. To do this, cut off the stem end of the aubergine (keep top for a lid) and hollow out the fruit with a spoon or knife, leaving a thick shell – be careful not to break the skin. Dice flesh, sprinkle them and inside of aubergine shell with salt. Put shell open-end-down into a colander and leave to drain for about 1 hour (stand colander on a plate to catch the dark juices).

Heat oven – 200°C/400°F/gas 6–7.

For the filling: Peel and chop onion and fresh garlic. Wash and chop tomato. Heat 1 tblsp oil in a small saucepan over a moderate heat and fry onion and garlic for 3–4 minutes until soft but not brown. Stir in chopped tomato and scissor-snipped parsley. Mix well and remove from heat.

Rinse and dry aubergine and stir diced aubergine into onion mixture. Stuff aubergine shell with the filling and top with the aubergine lid. Stand aubergine carefully in a small oven-proof dish. Mix remainder of olive oil, lemon juice, sugar, salt and pepper and pour over aubergine. Add a little water to come nearly halfway up the fruit – ¼–½ cupful.

Cover with a lid or piece of foil and bake in the hot oven for 15 minutes, then reduce heat to 160°C/325°F/gas 3–4 for a further 45 minutes. Or to cook in the traditional way, simmer the aubergine in the oil and water in a small saucepan on top of the stove for about an hour.

Remove from heat and carefully arrange on a serving dish. Serve hot or cold.

SUNDAY LUNCH, ROASTS
AND BURGERS

When my daughter stopped eating meat, the dish she missed most was her Sunday roast, but the withdrawal symptoms disappeared when we discovered nut and lentil roasts. These are delicious served with the roast potatoes and vegetables cooked for the rest of the family (but do remember to roast the potatoes in a separate tin, not round the meat!), and topped with a rich vegetarian gravy. My other personal favourites in this section are the vege-sausages, do try them.

I usually prepare at least double the quantity when making roasts, burgers and sausages as they freeze so well. I put uncooked portions of roasts in individual dishes, which can be quickly defrosted and cooked when needed. Burgers and sausages are wrapped individually in plastic film before freezing. They can then be defrosted and cooked in a similar way to commercially frozen ones, and served with vegetables or in a bun, topped with ketchup or grilled cheese, like all the best "fast food".

NUT ROAST   *2 portions*

"The" traditional vegetarian meal that everyone has heard of.

It is worth making at least 2 portions at a time of this recipe, as cold nut roast is tasty too. The second portion can be frozen, uncooked for use later.

Preparation and cooking time: 45 minutes – individual dishes
60 minutes – larger dishes.

1 onion
1 stick celery
4 oz/100g/1 very full cup mixed nuts, roughly chopped (a
**   processor or liquidiser is useful for this)**
2 large fresh tomatoes   or
Use the tomatoes from a small (7 oz/230g) can of tomatoes
**   (you can drink the juice as an aperitif)**
1 tblsp oil and a knob butter for frying
3 oz/75g/3 full cups fresh wholemeal breadcrumbs
Salt, pepper
½ tsp mixed herbs
Pinch of chilli powder
1 egg
Piece of foil for covering dishes

Grease 2 individual dishes or 1 larger tin (foil dishes are useful for this).

Heat oven – 200°C/400°F/gas 6–7.

Peel and chop onion, wash and chop celery, chop nuts and

chop fresh or tinned tomatoes.

Heat oil and butter in a large frying pan or saucepan over a moderate heat and fry onion and celery gently for 4–5 minutes until softened but not browned. Remove from heat. Add nuts, breadcrumbs, chopped tomatoes, salt, pepper, herbs and chilli powder.

Beat egg in a small basin or cup and stir into mixture. Taste, and adjust seasoning and herbs if necessary.

Spoon into well-greased tins and cover lightly with greased cooking foil.

Bake in the hot oven
for 20–30 minutes, removing foil after 15 mins – small tins or 45–60 minutes, removing foil after 30 mins – large tins. Serve with tomato sauce (see page 178) or gravy (see page 175).

This dish freezes well before baking. Defrost thoroughly before cooking as above.

LENTIL ROAST   *2 helpings*

This makes a good "Sunday Lunch" and can be served with cranberry sauce, red-currant jelly, apple sauce or mint sauce, and vege gravy (see page 175), to fit in with the menu for the rest of the family.

Lentil roast freezes well, so I make double quantity and put extra individual portions in the freezer for later, defrosting them when needed, before baking.

Preparation and cooking time: 45 minutes, individual dishes
55 minutes, larger dish.

Little oil or butter for greasing tins
1–2 tblsp dried breadcrumbs (optional)
4 oz/100g/4 heaped tblsp dry split red lentils
1 cup/$\frac{1}{4}$ pt/142ml water
$\frac{1}{2}$ tsp dried herbs
1 small onion
2 or 3 medium-size mushrooms
2 oz/50g Cheddar cheese
1 egg
1 oz/25g/1 cup fresh wholemeal breadcrumbs
Few sprigs of parsley and/or chives
1 tsp lemon juice
Salt, pepper

Grease very well 2 individual foil dishes or a larger dish. If liked, sprinkle dried breadcrumbs over base and sides.

Wash and drain lentils, put into a saucepan with the water and dried herbs. Bring to the boil, then lower the heat and simmer with the lid off the pan for 15–20 minutes, until the liquid is all absorbed and the lentils are tender.

While lentils are cooking, heat oven – 190°C/375°F/gas 5–6.

Peel and finely chop onion, wash and chop mushrooms, grate cheese, and beat egg in a cup with a fork.

Remove lentils from heat when cooked, mix in chopped onion, mushrooms, grated cheese, fresh breadcrumbs, washed scissor-snipped parsley and/or chives and lemon juice. Gradually add beaten egg, to make a soft but not runny mixture (you may not need quite all the egg). Season with salt and pepper.

Spoon mixture into prepared tins or dish. Lightly cover with foil. Freeze any spare dishes at this stage.

Bake in hot oven for 25 minutes – individual dishes
                    35 minutes – larger dish.
Remove foil for last 10–15 minutes of cooking time.

CHEESY PUD

2 servings

A quickly made savoury which can be frozen uncooked, ready to pop into the oven when needed.

Preparation and cooking time: 30–40 minutes.

1 small onion
2 oz/50g cheese – Cheddar or Edam – grated
1 tsp Parmesan
2 oz/50g/2 not-quite-full cups wholemeal breadcrumbs
1 egg
Salt, pepper
½ tsp mustard
7 fl oz/200ml/1¼ cups milk
Few sprigs of parsley and/or chives

Heat oven – 200°C/400°F/gas 6–7. Grease 2 individual oven-proof dishes or one larger dish.

Peel and finely chop onion and put into a bowl. Add grated cheese and breadcrumbs. Beat egg in a small basin with salt, pepper and mustard and stir into breadcrumb mixture adding milk and washed, scissor-snipped herbs. Mix well (it will be quite runny) and pour into the well-greased dish or dishes.

Bake for 20–30 minutes until set.

Serve hot with a crispy salad or green vegetables.

If cooking a frozen pudding it is best to defrost it before putting into the oven. If you must cook from frozen, allow 10–15 minutes extra cooking time and, if it starts getting too brown, cover with a lid of cooking foil.

MUSHROOM LAYERS *1 portion*

This dish freezes very well, so I usually make double the quantity and freeze one portion uncooked, ready for a quickly prepared meal in the future. It is best defrosted before cooking.

Preparation and cooking time: 35 minutes.

1 oz/25g butter
Little vegetable oil for frying
2 oz/50g/2 cupfuls fresh wholemeal breadcrumbs
2 oz/50g/2 really heaped tblsp mixed, chopped nuts
1 small onion
2 oz/50g mushrooms
2 oz/50g tomatoes, fresh or canned – (1 or 2 tomatoes according to size)
¼ small green pepper
Salt, pepper, pinch of mixed herbs
1 tsp sesame seeds (optional)
Little bit extra butter

Heat oven – 190°C/375°F/gas 5–6.
  Heat butter and oil in a frying pan and fry breadcrumbs and nuts together over a medium heat, stirring until crisp and golden (4–5 minutes). Remove from heat.
  Peel and chop onion, fry in a little oil in a saucepan over a low heat for 3–4 minutes until soft.
  Wash and slice mushrooms, wash and chop tomatoes and pepper, and stir into onion. Season with salt and pepper and mixed herbs, and simmer gently for 3–4 minutes.
  Grease a small deep dish, and put a layer of breadcrumb mixture in the bottom, cover with the vegetable mixture and then top with the rest of the breadcrumb and nut mixture.

Sprinkle with the sesame seeds, if liked.

Dot with the extra butter.

Bake in the hot oven for 15 minutes until nice and crispy on top.

Serve hot with a green salad and jacket potato.

For a change, use sunflower seeds mixed in with the nuts and breadcrumbs.

NUTBURGERS   *2 larger or 4 small burgers*

This makes a tasty vegetarian "beefburger" and is a life-saver for those with withdrawal symptoms from the burger bars! Serve in fresh bread rolls with ketchup; or as a Cheddar burger, topped with a slice of cheese after frying, and then toasted under a hot grill; or eat with potato salad, green salad and Bev's barbecue sauce (see page 180). Can be cooked over a barbecue or in a frying pan, or on a flat oiled griddle, but not too successful on a grid. Raw burgers can be frozen, individually wrapped, for later use.

Preparation and cooking time: 15 minutes plus cooling time before shaping.

1 small onion
1 stick of celery
1 tblsp oil and a little butter for frying
2 tsp cornflour or flour
½ vege stock cube
½ cup/2 fl oz/70ml water
4 oz/100g/1 full cup mixed nuts (cashew nuts, peanuts, walnuts, Brazil nuts) finely chopped. You can use the mixed, ready chopped nuts.
2 oz/50g/2 cups fresh wholemeal breadcrumbs
1–2 tsp mixed herbs

1 tsp soy sauce
1 tsp Worcester sauce
½ tsp yeast extract
Pinch of chilli powder
Salt, pepper
3–4 tblsp dried breadcrumbs } For coating
1–2 tblsp vegetable oil   } and frying

Peel and finely chop onion. Wash and finely chop celery.
Heat oil and butter in a pan over a medium heat, add onion
and celery and fry for 4–5 minutes until soft and lightly
browned.

In a cup or small basin mix cornflour or flour and
crumbled stock cube to a runny paste with 1 tblsp of the
water. Stir in rest of water and add to onion mixture. Stir
over gentle heat until sauce thickens. Remove from heat.

Add nuts, fresh breadcrumbs, herbs, sauces, yeast extract,
chilli powder and season with salt and pepper. Mix well
together.

Leave to cool, with lid off pan. (If you're in a hurry, turn
mixture onto a cold plate and put in fridge for a few
minutes.)

When mixture is firm enough to handle, divide into 2 large
or 4 smaller equal-size portions and shape into flat, round
burgers about ¾"/2cm thick.

Put dried breadcrumbs on a plate, and press the
nutburgers onto the dried crumbs to coat them.

Heat oil in a frying pan over a moderate heat and fry
burgers for 2–3 minutes on each side.

VEGE SAUSAGE   *Makes 4–6 according to size*

You can finely chop or grate the nuts for this recipe (easier if you have a liquidiser or food processor) or buy ready chopped mixed nuts.

Preparation and cooking time: 15 minutes plus ½ hour standing time if possible.

½ **small onion**
2 oz/50g/2 very heaped tblsp cashew nuts } **You need 4 oz/**
2 oz/50/2 very heaped tblsp walnuts } **100g altogether**
or
4 oz/100g/4 very heaped tblsp mixed chopped nuts
2 oz/50g Cheddar or Edam cheese
1 oz/25g/4 tblsp wholemeal or granary breadcrumbs
Pinch of curry powder or cayenne pepper (optional)
½ **tsp mixed herbs**
Salt, pepper
Little egg for mixing
1–2 tblsp vegetable oil for frying

Peel and grate or very finely chop onion. Grate or chop nuts. Grate cheese.

Put onion, breadcrumbs, nuts and cheese in a basin, and mix well with curry powder or cayenne pepper (if used), herbs, salt and pepper.

Beat egg in a small basin or cup, with a fork. Add egg to nut mixture a teaspoonful at a time, mixing after each addition and pressing it together to form a stiff mixture like Plasticine! (you may not need very much egg). Divide into 4–6 equal pieces and "roly-poly" pieces to make sausages. The sausages get firmer and easier to cook without crumbling if left in a cool place for half an hour.

Heat a little oil in a frying pan over a moderate heat and fry sausages gently for 3–5 minutes, turning frequently to brown evenly on all sides.

Drain on kitchen paper, serve hot with potatoes and vegetables or baked beans, or cold as a snack with ketchup, sauce or dips.

For a party, double the quantity of the mixture and shape into tiny "cocktail" sausages. Fry, drain well and serve cold on cocktail sticks with dips, see avocado dip (page 188) or tomato sauce (page 178).

These sausages can be wrapped, uncooked, individually in plastic wrap and deep frozen. They defrost very quickly ready for cooking when needed.

EGG AND MUSHROOM BURGERS

2–4 burgers

A tasty burger, quite a change from the more usual "nutty" recipe, and quite nutritious with its high egg content. Can be served in a bun with chips and ketchup or with fresh vegetables, home-made sauce or gravy as a main meal.

Preparation and cooking time: 35–40 minutes.

1 egg
Salt, pepper
1 small onion
1 clove of fresh garlic or ¼ tsp garlic powder (optional)
4 oz/100g mushrooms
1 tblsp vegetable oil
2 tsp cornflour or flour
2 tblsp water
¼ tsp yeast extract
½ tsp vegetable extract
6 heaped tblsp/1 very full cupful wholemeal breadcrumbs
Little lemon juice or Worcester sauce
Few sprigs of fresh parsley

Coating:
1–2 cups/2 oz/50g wholemeal breadcrumbs
1 egg
Vegetable oil for frying

Hard boil egg (cook in gently boiling salted water for 10 minutes, drain and plunge egg into cold water to cool). Peel egg, rinse off all the bits of shell, dry and chop finely.

Peel and finely chop onion and fresh garlic if used. Wash, drain and slice mushrooms. Heat vegetable oil in a saucepan over a moderate heat and fry onion and garlic for 3–4 minutes until soft but not brown, add sliced mushrooms and continue cooking for a further 1–2 minutes until mushrooms are soft. Stir in cornflour or flour, water, yeast extract, vegetable extract and continue cooking gently for another 2–3 minutes, stirring well to make a thick sauce. Remove pan from heat and stir in breadcrumbs and chopped egg. Season to taste with salt, pepper and lemon juice or Worcester sauce and mix in washed scissor-snipped parsley. Leave to cool.

Sprinkle a little flour on a clean work surface, divide mixture into 2 large or 4 medium pieces and shape into burgers. Pour breadcrumbs for coating into a soup bowl, beat egg and pour into another dish. Dip burgers in egg and then coat thickly with the breadcrumbs. Heat vegetable oil in a frying pan over a moderate heat. Shallow fry them in $1/4''/1/2$ cm deep oil for 3–4 minutes on each side, until a lovely golden brown.

Drain well on kitchen paper and serve hot.

Raw burgers can be frozen, individually wrapped, for later use.

CHEESY MILLET CUTLETS

Makes 2 large cutlets

An unusual variation on the "burger" theme, very

nourishing and tasty. I usually make double the quantity, wrap the extra cutlets separately in plastic film and freeze them for "instant" meals and snacks in the future.

Preparation and cooking time: 45 minutes (plus cooling time).

½ small onion
1 small clove of garlic or ¼ tsp garlic powder
1 or 2 rings of green pepper
1 stick of celery
2 oz/50g/2 heaped tblsp millet
1¼ cups/6 fl oz/177ml boiling water
½ vegetable stock cube
¼ tsp vegetable extract
½ tsp mixed herbs
¼ tsp cayenne pepper or curry powder
2 tsp cooked or canned sweetcorn
1 oz/25g Cheddar or Edam cheese, grated
½ tsp Parmesan cheese, grated (optional)
Few sprigs of parsley and/or chives
Salt, pepper
Little flour for shaping
1–2 tblsp vegetable oil for frying

Peel and finely chop onion and fresh garlic. Wash and chop green pepper and celery, and put all the vegetables into a medium-sized saucepan.

Add washed millet (rinse in a sieve), boiling water, crumbled stock cube, vegetable extract, herbs, cayenne pepper or curry powder and stir well. Bring to the boil, reduce heat and simmer for about 20 minutes, stirring occasionally until all the water is absorbed. Watch carefully for the last few minutes to make sure it doesn't burn. Remove from heat.

Stir in sweetcorn and grated cheeses. Wash and scissor-snip parsley and chives into mixture. Season with salt and pepper. Stir well and leave to cool until firm enough to handle.

When cool and firm, divide into 2 even-sized lumps and shape into cutlet or burger shapes (you may need to use a little flour to stop it sticking), using your hands or a wide-bladed knife.

Heat a little oil in a frying pan over a moderate heat and fry cutlets for 3–4 minutes on each side, until golden brown and crispy.

Serve hot, with tomato sauce (see page 178), or mustard sauce (see page 179) or gravy (see page 175), potatoes and a green vegetable salad, or with baked beans and a bread roll for a quick meal.

T.S.P. – TEXTURED SOYA PROTEIN

A very useful standby in the vegetarian store cupboard, cheaper than meat but resembling mince or stewed steak when hydrated. Follow the instructions on individual packets. Minced T.S.P. is generally hydrated (mixed with liquid to change it from its dried state) in a few minutes, while the chunks take 20–30 minutes. Adding a vegetable stock cube, vegetable extract or a little yeast extract to the water gives extra goodness and flavour to the finished dish.

The hydrated T.S.P. can be used in exactly the same way as raw mince or stewing steak, with the advantage that it does not take as long to cook as "proper" meat: 5–10 minutes for mince, 20–30 minutes for chunks.

To hydrate T.S.P. – 1 serving

Minced T.S.P.
1 oz/25g/nearly ½ cup minced T.S.P.
¾ cup/4 fl oz/115ml water
½ vegetable stock cube or ½ tsp vegetable or yeast extract
2 tsp vegetable oil

Put all ingredients into a small saucepan, crumbling the
stock cube. Bring gently to the boil, then simmer for 2–3
minutes until the water is absorbed and the mixture
resembles mince.

T.S.P. Chunks
½ cup/1 oz/25g T.S.P. chunks
1 cup/¼ pt/142ml water
½ vegetable stock cube or ½ tsp vegetable or yeast extract
2 tsp vegetable oil

Put all ingredients into a small saucepan, crumbling the
stock cube. Bring gently to the boil and simmer for 20–30
minutes until the water is absorbed and the mixture
resembles stewing steak.

T.S.P. AND MUSHROOM PIE

1 individual pie

I try to make this recipe in at least double the quantity,
making several individual pies, either in foil dishes or small
Pyrex dishes. These pies freeze well and are handy for a quick
meal. Any spare gravy can be frozen in a little plastic tub to
serve with the pie.

Preparation and cooking time: 60 minutes.

T.S.P.
½ cup/1 oz/25g T.S.P. chunks
½ vegetable stock cube
1 cup/¼ pt/142ml water
2 tsp vegetable oil

Pastry
1 frozen puff pastry "leaf" or small piece of puff pastry (you
can buy packets of individual sheets of puff pastry)

Filling
½ onion
1 small carrot
3 or 4 mushrooms
2 tsp vegetable oil
1 tblsp sherry or wine or cider
½ vegetable stock cube
¼ tsp vegetable extract
½ cup/2½ fl oz/70ml water
½ tsp mixed herbs
Salt, pepper

1–2 tsp milk for brushing pastry

Gravy
Liquid from cooking T.S.P. with the vegetables
½ tsp flour or cornflour
½ tsp gravy powder
1 tblsp sherry, wine or cold water

Hydrate T.S.P. chunks as on packet (see page 160).
Leave frozen pastry to defrost.
Peel and slice onion and carrot, wash and slice mushrooms.
Heat oil in saucepan, fry onion over a gentle heat for 3–4

minutes until soft. Add hydrated T.S.P., carrot and mushrooms and continue to fry gently for a further 2–3 minutes, adding sherry, wine or cider, if used.

Stir in crumbled stock cube, vegetable extract, water, herbs and seasoning. Bring slowly to the boil, reduce heat and simmer for 10–15 minutes with lid on, stirring occasionally until carrot is cooked (test with a knife).

Heat oven – 200°C/400°F/gas 6–7.

Remove soya and vegetable mixture from gravy using a slotted spoon and put into pie dish with 1 tblsp of the gravy. Roll out pastry ($\frac{1}{4}$″/$\frac{1}{2}$cm thick) if necessary, and cover the filling in the dish with the pastry, being careful to ease the pastry over the top and sides without stretching it, and cut to fit with a knife. Pinch edges to look pretty, roll scraps to make pastry leaves and decorate top of pie. Brush with milk and bake in the hot oven for 15–20 minutes until pastry is risen and golden.

Gravy – mix flour and cornflour and gravy powder to a runny paste with sherry, wine or cold water in a small pan. Stir in gravy saved from cooking the vegetables and bring to the boil, stirring all the time until it thickens.

T.S.P. GOULASH   *1 large helping*

Quick and easy to prepare for a vegetarian while making a beef goulash for the rest of the family.

Preparation and cooking time: 50 minutes.

T.S.P.
$\frac{1}{2}$ cup/1 oz/25g T.S.P. chunks (not mince)
1 cup/$\frac{1}{4}$ pt/142ml water
$\frac{1}{2}$ vegetable stock cube
2 tsp vegetable oil

Goulash

1 small onion
1 small carrot
$\frac{1}{2}$ small (7 oz/230g) can tomatoes or 2 fresh tomatoes
1 potato
1 tblsp cooking oil
$\frac{1}{2}$–1 tsp paprika pepper
1 tsp tomato purée or tomato ketchup
$\frac{1}{2}$ vegetable stock cube
$\frac{1}{4}$ tsp vegetable extract
$\frac{1}{2}$–1 cup/2$\frac{1}{2}$–5 fl oz/70–142ml water
$\frac{1}{2}$ tsp mixed herbs
Salt, pepper
2 tsp soured cream, cream or yoghurt
Parsley for garnish

Hydrate T.S.P. as directed on packet, see page 160.

While T.S.P. is simmering, peel and slice onion, peel and slice carrot thickly ($\frac{1}{4}$″/$\frac{1}{2}$cm rings), wash and chop fresh tomatoes, peel potato and cut into bite-sized chunks.

Heat oil in medium saucepan, fry onion over a medium heat for 3–4 minutes until softened. Add hydrated T.S.P. and carrot and mix gently with the onion over a low heat. Add paprika, then stir in canned or chopped fresh tomatoes, tomato purée or ketchup, crumbled stock cube, vegetable extract, $\frac{1}{2}$ cup water, herbs and seasoning. Add chunked potato and bring to the boil, stirring occasionally, then reduce heat and leave to simmer with lid on for 15–20 minutes stirring occasionally until potato is cooked (test with a knife). Add a little more water if it gets too dry; there should be plenty of gravy.

Serve in a deep plate or bowl, topped with cream, soured cream or yoghurt, and scissor-snipped washed parsley.

Eat with a hot granary roll or crispy French bread.

T.S.P. BOLOGNESE   *2 servings*

You might as well make 2 helpings, it saves a lot of time in the future and it's easier to simmer slightly larger quantities, they don't dry up while cooking as very small amounts do.

Preparation and cooking time: 30 minutes.

T.S.P.
2 oz/50g/1 almost-full cup minced T.S.P.
1½ cups/8 fl oz/225ml water
½ vegetable stock cube
1 tblsp vegetable oil

Sauce
1 small onion
1 clove of garlic or ¼ tsp minced garlic
1 small carrot
1 small (7 oz/230g) can tomatoes or 3–4 fresh tomatoes
1 tblsp vegetable oil
1 tblsp tomato purée or ketchup
½ vegetable stock cube and 1 cup/5 fl oz/142ml water, or 1 cup of tomato or vegetable soup
Salt, pepper
½ tsp mixed herbs
Dash of Worcester sauce
¼ tsp sugar

Hydrate T.S.P. (see page 160).

Peel and chop onion and fresh garlic. Peel and grate or finely chop carrot. Chop tomatoes.

Heat oil in a saucepan and fry onion and garlic over a moderate heat for 4–5 minutes until softened but not brown. Add T.S.P., carrot, tinned or fresh tomatoes (use juice from can as well), tomato purée or ketchup, crumbled stock cube and water, or canned soup, stirring well. Season with salt, pepper, herbs, Worcester sauce and sugar. Bring to the boil, then reduce heat and simmer, stirring occasionally for 10–15 minutes, adding a little more liquid if it seems too stiff, until a good thick sauce is made.

Freeze in individual portions for use later, if required.

Note: If using this sauce for lasagne, with "no cook" lasagne strips, add a little more liquid to make a runny sauce, as the lasagne absorbs the extra liquid while cooking.

T.S.P. CURRY   *Serves 1*

Curry freezes well, so if you have a deep freeze it makes sense to make double the quantity and freeze one portion in an individual container for future use.

Preparation and cooking time: 55 minutes – including hydrating T.S.P.

T.S.P.
½ cup/1 oz/25g T.S.P. chunks
1 cup/¼ pt/142ml water
½ vegetable stock cube
2 tsp vegetable oil

1 small onion
1 small apple
1 tsp lemon juice
1 tblsp vegetable oil
1–2 tsp curry powder – mild or hot according to taste
1–2 tomatoes, cut in quarters   *(continued overleaf)*

(T.S.P. Curry continued)

½ **vegetable stock cube and 1 cup boiling water**
or 1 cup vegetable soup
1 tsp tomato purée or ketchup
1 tsp sugar – brown or white
1 tsp sweet pickle or chutney
1 tblsp sultanas

Hydrate T.S.P. chunks as on packet, or see page 160.

Peel and chop onion. Peel and chop apple and sprinkle with lemon juice.

Heat oil in saucepan over a moderate heat and fry onion for 3–4 minutes until softened. Add the hydrolysed T.S.P. chunks, sprinkle curry powder over T.S.P. and stir for a few minutes over a moderate heat. Add chopped apple and tomato pieces and continue to fry for a further 2–3 minutes, stirring gently. Crumble stock cube in boiling water and add to the T.S.P. mixture, or add the soup. Stir in tomato purée or ketchup, sugar, pickle or chutney and washed, drained sultanas. Stir well and simmer gently with the lid on but stirring occasionally for 10–12 minutes until the vegetables are cooked.

Serve with plain boiled rice (see page 48), poppadums and side dishes (see page 121).

CHILLI   *Serves 1*

This is a convenient dish to make for both vegetarians and the non-converted by substituting T.S.P. for beef. It's easy to make the two recipes at the same time as long as you remember not to dip the meat spoon in the T.S.P. saucepan!

Chilli freezes well, so if possible double the ingredients and cook two portions.

Preparation and cooking time: 35 minutes.

T.S.P.
½ cup/1 oz/25g minced T.S.P.
¾ cup/4 fl oz/115ml water
½ vegetable stock cube or ½ tsp vegetable extract
2 tsp vegetable oil

1 small onion
1 clove of garlic or ¼ tsp garlic paste or powder
1 stick of celery
1 carrot
1 tomato – fresh or canned
1 tblsp vegetable oil for frying
½ level tsp chilli powder
1 tblsp tomato purée or ketchup
½–1 cup/2½–5 fl oz/70–142ml water
¼ vegetable stock cube
¼ tsp yeast extract
Salt, pepper
1 cup cooked kidney beans (canned or pre-cooked dried beans, see page 77)
Dash of Worcester sauce
Few drops of tabasco sauce

Hydrate T.S.P. (see page 160).
  Peel and chop onion and fresh garlic. Wash and chop celery. Peel and finely dice carrot. Slice tomato into chunks.
  Heat oil in a saucepan over a moderate heat and fry onion, garlic and celery for 4–5 minutes until softened but not brown. Add carrot and hydrated T.S.P. and continue to fry

gently, stirring all the time, for a further 2–3 minutes. Add tomato pieces, chilli powder, tomato purée or ketchup, water, crumbled stock cube, yeast extract, salt and pepper, and stir well. Add cooked kidney beans and bring to the boil, then reduce heat, cover pan and simmer for 10–15 minutes, stirring occasionally (adding a little extra water if it gets too dry), until a lovely thick sauce is produced. Taste and season with Worcester sauce and a few drops of tabasco (be wary of tabasco, a little goes a very long way!).

Serve chilli hot with boiled rice or poured over a jacket potato. Alternatively a bowl full of hot chilli with crusty bread rolls and a green salad makes a very satisfying supper dish.

SAVOURY SHEPHERD'S PIE   *Serves 1*

Another dish that's easy to make using T.S.P. while making a conventional Shepherd's Pie for the rest of the family. Suitable for freezing, to make an "instant" meal in the future.

Preparation and cooking time: 40–45 minutes.

T.S.P.
½ cup/1 oz/25g minced T.S.P.
¾ cup/4 fl oz/115ml water
½ vegetable stock cube or ½ tsp vegetable extract
2 tsp vegetable oil

1 small onion
1 tblsp vegetable oil
1 tblsp wine, beer or sherry
1 tsp tomato purée or ketchup

Shake of Worcester sauce
1 tsp sweet pickle or chutney
¼ vegetable stock cube and ½–1 cup/2½–5 fl oz/70–142ml
      water
or ½–1 cup/2½–5 fl oz/70–142ml vegetable soup
¼ tsp yeast extract
½ tsp mixed herbs

Topping
2–3 potatoes
½ oz/12g butter or margarine
1–2 oz/25–50g Cheddar or Edam cheese, grated
1 tomato – sliced

Hydrate T.S.P. (see page 160).

Peel and chop onion. Heat oil in saucepan over a moderate heat and fry onion gently for 2–3 minutes until softened. Stir in hydrated T.S.P., wine, beer or sherry, sauces, pickle, crumbled stock cube and water or vegetable soup, yeast extract and herbs. Bring to the boil, then reduce heat and simmer for 10–12 minutes, stirring occasionally, adding a little more liquid if the mixture gets too dry.

Meanwhile, peel potatoes and cut them into thick slices, cook in boiling salted water for 7–10 minutes until soft. Drain well, and mash with a potato masher or fork. Add butter and beat until creamy, then beat in grated cheese, saving a little to sprinkle on top of the pie.

Pour T.S.P. mixture into oven-proof pie dish, cover with the cheesy potato and fork down smoothly. Sprinkle with reserved cheese and decorate with tomato slices. Cook under a hot grill for 2–3 minutes until bubbly and golden brown or put on the top shelf of a hot oven – 200°C/400°F/gas 6–7 – for 5–10 minutes until brown.

You can make this in advance and keep (uncooked) in the fridge or freezer until needed. Heat in the hot oven for 15–20 minutes as above.

ONE-STEP CASSEROLE OR STEW

1 generous helping

The T.S.P. chunks are hydrated while the casserole or stew is cooking, so the recipe will seem very runny at the beginning but a lot of the liquid will be absorbed during cooking, leaving a super savoury gravy. If you're making a meat and vegetable casserole for the rest of the family, you can use any selection from those vegetables for this recipe.

Preparation and cooking time: 50–60 minutes.

1 small onion
1 clove of garlic or $\frac{1}{4}$ tsp garlic granules
1 stick of celery
1 small carrot
2–3 mushrooms
1 tblsp vegetable oil
$\frac{1}{2}$ small (7 oz/230g) can tomatoes
$\frac{1}{2}$ cup/1 oz/25g T.S.P. chunks
1 vegetable stock cube or $\frac{1}{2}$ tsp vegetable extract
$\frac{1}{4}$ tsp yeast extract
1 tsp tomato purée or ketchup
$\frac{1}{2}$ tsp mixed herbs
Salt, pepper
1 tsp flour or cornflour
$\frac{1}{2}$ tsp gravy powder
2–3 cups/10–15 fl oz/284–426ml water and/or wine, cider or
     beer

Peel and slice onion and fresh garlic, wash and chop celery into 1″/2½cm lengths, peel and slice carrot into rings, wash mushrooms and slice if large.

Heat oil in a saucepan or casserole over a moderate heat, and fry onion, garlic and celery for 4–5 minutes until softened but not brown. Add carrot and mushrooms and continue to cook for 2–3 minutes, then add canned tomatoes (fruit and juice) and T.S.P. chunks, and mix well. Stir in crumbled stock cube or vegetable extract, yeast extract, tomato purée or ketchup, mixed herbs, salt and pepper.

Put flour or cornflour and gravy powder into a small basin and mix to a smooth paste with 1 tblsp alcohol or cold water. Add 2 cups of liquid and stir into vegetable mixture. Bring slowly to the boil, stirring gently. Put the covered casserole into a moderate oven – 170°C/325°F/gas 3–4 – for 30–40 minutes, or simmer saucepan over a very low heat with the lid on for 30–40 minutes, stirring occasionally until the vegetables are cooked and the gravy has thickened. Add a little more liquid during cooking if the casserole or stew seems to be getting too dry.

STUFFED PEPPERS   *1–2 peppers*

A nice family supper to make when peppers are cheap; as prices vary quite a lot during the year it's worth watching out for bargains. Allow 1–2 peppers per person according to size (of both peppers and persons!), and use T.S.P. or, for non-vegetarians, minced beef for the stuffing.

Preparation and cooking time: 35 minutes.

T.S.P.
½ cup/1 oz/25g minced T.S.P.
¾ cup/4 fl oz/115ml water
½ vegetable stock cube or ½ tsp vegetable extract
2 tsp vegetable oil

1 small onion
1 clove of garlic or ¼ tsp garlic powder
1 small tomato, fresh or canned
1–2 mushrooms
1 tblsp vegetable oil for frying
2 tsp tomato purée or ketchup
¼ stock cube
¼–½ cup/1–2½ fl oz/35–70ml boiling water
1 tblsp raw rice or 2 tblsp left-over cooked rice
¼ tsp yeast extract
Salt, pepper
¼ tsp mixed herbs
1–2 green peppers
1 oz/25g grated cheese – Cheddar or Edam

Hydrate T.S.P. (see page 160).

Peel and chop onion and garlic, wash and chop fresh tomato and mushrooms. Heat oil in a saucepan and fry onion and garlic gently for 2–3 minutes until softened. Stir in hydrated T.S.P., chopped tomato (canned or fresh), chopped mushrooms, tomato purée or ketchup, crumbled stock cube and boiling water, and washed raw rice. Continue to simmer over a moderate heat with the lid off for 10 minutes, stirring occasionally. The stock should be almost completely absorbed. If using cooked rice, stir it in now and season with salt, pepper and herbs.

Heat oven – 180°C/350°F/gas 4–5. Grease an oven-proof dish. Slice the tops off peppers (and keep the tops), remove seeds and wash peppers.

Remove filling mixture from heat and strain off any excess liquid (the mixture should be fairly moist, but not swimming in gravy). Fill peppers with the mixture, top with grated cheese, put on lids and place peppers carefully in the greased dish. Bake in the hot oven for 15–20 minutes. The peppers can be made in advance and stood in the fridge until required.

SAUCES, DRESSINGS AND DIPS

Sauces are very important in the vegetarian menu as they can transform an ordinary cooked vegetable into a really super meal.

Lovely home-made sauces are delicious, cheap and quick and easy to make. Some sauces can be used as a sauce or a dip, served hot or cold.

Most sauces and gravies freeze well (with the exception of mayonnaise which separates if frozen) and can be kept in the freezer in individual portions (it's also easier to make a larger amount of gravy than to fiddle about trying to make a spoonful), but do remember to make sure that the pre-frozen sauce is re-cooked properly, not just warmed before serving.

The dressings will keep in a screw-top jar in the fridge, to use when needed and the dips can be served as individual starters, or in large bowls at a party.

VEGE GRAVY

½ pt/284ml – 2–4 servings

Preparation and cooking time: 5 minutes.

A life-saver for vegetarians who thought they could never have gravy again!

1 tsp flour or cornflour (use more or less flour for thicker or
       thinner gravy)
½ tsp gravy powder
½ glass wine, sherry or beer (optional) or cold water
½ tsp yeast extract
½ vegetable stock cube
1 tsp tomato purée or ketchup
1 tsp soy sauce
1 large cup or mug hot water (use vegetable water if possible)
Dab butter

Mix flour or cornflour and gravy powder to a runny paste with the alcohol or cold water, in a small saucepan.

Add yeast extract, crumbled stock cube, tomato purée or ketchup and soy sauce, and stir well.

Mix in the hot water or vegetable water, stirring well to prevent gravy going lumpy. Bring to the boil, still stirring, and beat in butter, simmer for 2–3 minutes until thick and smooth.

Left-over gravy can be frozen in small, lidded plastic pots ready to defrost, heat and serve another day.

WHITE SAUCE

1–2 Servings

A quick way to make a basic sauce, to which you can add

other ingredients or flavourings as required.

Preparation and cooking time: 5 minutes.

2 tsp cornflour or flour
¼ pt/142ml/1 cup milk
½ oz/12g butter or margarine
Salt, pepper

Put cornflour or flour into a small basin and mix it to a runny paste with 1 tblsp of the milk. Boil rest of the milk in a small saucepan, and pour it onto the well-stirred flour, stirring all the time. Pour mixture back into the saucepan, return to the heat and bring back to the boil, stirring all the time with a wooden spoon until the sauce thickens. Beat in butter or margarine, and season with salt and pepper.

Cheese Sauce
Grate 1–2 oz/25–50g Cheddar, Edam or other hard-type cheese (the strong flavoured ones give a more tasty sauce). Add to the white sauce with the butter or margarine, and add a dash of mustard with the seasoning.

Parsley Sauce
Wash and drain a handful of fresh sprigs of parsley. Chop or scissor-snip them finely and add to the sauce with the seasoning.

ONION SAUCE   *1–2 Servings*

This is a quick and easy method and makes a tasty sauce, delicious poured over cauliflower, marrow or most other vegetables.

Preparation and cooking time: 25 minutes.

1 onion
¼ pt/142ml/1 cup water
2 tsp cornflour or flour
¼ pt/142ml/1 cup milk
Knob of butter
Salt, pepper

Peel and finely chop onion. Put into a small saucepan with the cup of water. Bring to the boil, then lower heat and simmer gently for 10–15 minutes until onion is soft. In a small bowl mix cornflour or flour to a paste with 1 tblsp of the milk. Gradually add this to the onion mixture, stirring all the time as the mixture thickens. Add more milk until the sauce is just thick enough – not runny, but not like blancmange. Beat in the butter and season with salt and plenty of pepper. Serve hot.

MUSHROOM SAUCE   *1–2 Servings*

A quickly made, tasty sauce with roasts, burgers or vegetables, or it can be used as a change from gravy.

Preparation and cooking time: 10 minutes.

2 oz/50g mushrooms
½ oz/12g butter or margarine
2 tsp cornflour or flour
¼ pt/142ml/1 cup milk
Salt, pepper
Shake of cayenne pepper

Wash and thinly slice mushrooms. Melt butter or margarine in a saucepan over a low heat, add sliced mushrooms and fry gently for 2–3 minutes until soft. Remove from heat.

Put cornflour or flour into a small basin, and mix to a runny paste with 1 tblsp of the milk. Stir this into the mushrooms, gradually mixing in the rest of the milk. Return pan to heat, bring gently to the boil and cook until the sauce thickens, stirring all the time. Season well with salt, pepper and a little cayenne pepper. Serve hot.

HOME-MADE TOMATO SAUCE

½ pint (2 generous portions)

A nice spicy sauce. Good instead of gravy with nut roast, lentil roast etc.

Preparation and cooking time: 30 minutes.

1 onion
Little oil and butter for frying
1 small (7 oz/230g) can tomatoes (use the juice as well)
or ½ lb/200g fresh tomatoes – 3–4 large tomatoes
½ tsp soy sauce
1 tsp tomato purée or ketchup
½ tsp sugar
½ tsp mixed herbs
Pinch of garlic
Salt, pepper

Peel and finely chop onion. Heat oil and butter in a saucepan over a low heat, and fry onion gently for 4–5 minutes until transparent.

Chop fresh tomatoes, or break up canned tomatoes, add to onion and stir in soy sauce, tomato purée or ketchup, sugar, herbs and seasoning.

Bring to the boil, stirring well, then reduce heat and simmer gently for 10 minutes, stirring occasionally (it may splash a bit, so cover with a lid).

Allow to cool slightly, then liquidise if you want a smooth sauce, but it can be used without liquidising if you haven't got a liquidiser or a blender, it's just as tasty.

This sauce freezes well, and can be frozen in individual portions, to be defrosted and used when needed. If you have a freezer, it's no more trouble to make double the quantity than a smaller amount.

MUSTARD SAUCE   *Serves 1–2*

Use with vegeburger, millet cutlets etc., or as a change from gravy with nut or lentil roasts.

Preparation and cooking time: 5 minutes.

1 tsp flour or cornflour
1 tblsp wine, sherry, beer or cold water
½ vegetable stock cube
1 cup boiling water (use vegetable stock if available)
1 tsp mild French mustard (whole seed type is best)
2 tblsp cream or yoghurt
Salt, pepper
Dab of butter (optional, see note at end of recipe)

Blend flour or cornflour to a paste with the alcohol or cold water, in a little basin. Add crumbled stock cube and boiling water, and stir well. Pour into the frying pan (if you have not been cooking vegeburgers, etc., see overleaf) and mix well with the fat in the pan. Stir with a wooden spoon over a moderate heat until sauce thickens.

Stir in mustard and mix well.

Reduce heat, stir in cream or yoghurt and season well with salt and pepper, adding more mustard if necessary. Do not let the sauce boil once cream or yoghurt is added, or it may curdle; just let it warm through.

Serve hot with vegeburgers, nut roasts etc.

Note: This sauce can be made in a small saucepan if you've not been using the frying pan. Add a dab of butter with the mustard if there is no left-over fat in the frying pan to be used.

BEV'S BARBECUE SAUCE   *1 large mugful*

Equally good with vegetarian or meaty grills.

Preparation and cooking time: 25–30 minutes.

1 large onion
1 apple – eating or cooking
1–2 tomatoes
1 tblsp vegetable oil
2 tsp vinegar
1 cup/¼ pt/142ml beer
2 tsp sugar – white or brown
1 tblsp sultanas (optional, but nice), washed and drained
1 tblsp sweet pickle and/or 1 tblsp tomato ketchup
Dash of Worcester sauce and/or tabasco and/or soy sauce

This is very much a "taste as you go" recipe. Add a little more of the ingredients as the sauce is cooking until a nice, thick, tasty sauce is obtained.

Peel and chop onion, peel, core and chop apple, wash and chop tomatoes.

Heat oil in a smallish saucepan over a low heat, and fry onion, stirring well until softened but not browned, about 5 minutes.

Add chopped apple and tomato and cook for a further 2–3 minutes, then gradually stir in vinegar and beer, and leave to simmer for about 10 minutes with the lid off, stirring quite often until sauce begins to thicken.

Now the fun starts – add sugar, sultanas, pickle, tomato ketchup, Worcester, tabasco and/or soy sauce, stirring over a gentle heat and tasting as you go along.

Continue to simmer for a further 5–10 minutes, stirring well so that it does not burn on the base of the pan, until sauce is of a thick, spreading consistency and tastes really good.

Serve hot or cold. Extra sauce will keep for a few days in a clean, covered jar in the fridge.

MAYONNAISE   *1 generous cupful*

Even if you've never tried to make mayonnaise before, do have a go at this recipe, it's quite delicious and although easier to make with an electric mixer, it can be made using a whisk or wooden spoon. The plain mayonnaise is super with salads, jacket potatoes, hard-boiled eggs etc. or as a base for dips, flavoured with tomato purée, curry or garlic, or mixed with Stilton cheese or mashed avocado pear.

Preparation time: 15–20 minutes.

All the ingredients must be at room temperature or the

mixture may curdle. Take the egg from the fridge at least 30 minutes beforehand.

1 egg yolk
2 tsp lemon juice or vinegar (wine vinegar is best)
Large pinch of salt
Small pinch of dry mustard or a spot of made-up mustard
Shake of pepper
¼ pt/142ml/1 cup olive oil (you can use any vegetable oil, but
**   the flavour is not quite the same)**

Beat egg yolk in a small basin with 1 tsp of the vinegar or lemon juice, and the seasonings. Gradually add the oil, a drop at a time at first (drip it off the teaspoon), beating all the time. As the sauce thickens the oil can be added faster, beating hard until all the oil is mixed in.

Taste and adjust flavour, by adding more vinegar or lemon juice. If it is still too thick, add a teaspoon of warm water (room temperature). The mayonnaise should be lovely, thick and creamy.

If by any chance the mayonnaise curdles and doesn't thicken, don't panic. Separate another egg (at room temperature) and then beat the curdled mayonnaise, a drop at a time, into the new yolk, then gradually add any remaining oil, beating all the time.

Mayonnaise is best made with the help of a friend, so that one of you whisks whilst the other drips the oil!

It will keep for a few days in a covered jar or dish in the fridge.

VINAIGRETTE (FRENCH) DRESSING

An essential sauce to have to hand in the fridge (keep in a

small, screw-top jar) as it keeps for weeks in a cool place, and is the most widely used dressing for all kinds of salads. It's very quick to make and you can add your favourite flavourings to the basic recipe – use flavoured vinegar or plain lemon juice, add a pinch of garlic or herbs, or use honey instead of sugar. Olive or walnut oils give the best flavour, but are expensive. Other vegetable oils are quite acceptable, being cheaper but have rather less flavour.

For one serving
2 tsp olive or vegetable oil
1 tsp wine vinegar or lemon juice
Pinch of salt, pepper, mustard, sugar

Put all ingredients in a cup or small basin, stir vigorously with a teaspoon until well mixed. Pour over salad, turning all the ingredients in the dressing.

To make a jarful
Use proportions of 2 lots of oil to 1 lot of vinegar. Take a small, clean screwtop jar or wide-necked bottle. Pour into it:

½ cup/2½ fl oz/70ml olive oil or vegetable oil
¼ cup/1 fl oz/35ml vinegar or lemon juice
¼ tsp salt
¼ tsp pepper
¼ tsp mustard
½–1 tsp sugar (according to taste)

Screw lid on firmly. Shake well for 2–3 minutes until thoroughly mixed. Store in the fridge and shake again before use. If it solidifies, stand the jar in warm water for a few minutes before use, or remove from fridge and stand in a warm room for half-an-hour, until dressing is runny again.

Add any flavourings when you mix the ingredients. Wine vinegar has a less harsh flavour than malt vinegar.

SLIMMER'S SALAD DRESSING

1–2 Servings

A quickly made dressing for salads which does not contain any oil. If the honey is too thick, stand the open jar in a pan with a little hot water over a low heat for a few minutes, until the honey melts.

Preparation time: 5 minutes.

2 tblsp runny honey
2 tblsp lemon juice
Salt, pepper

Put honey into a small basin or cup. Gradually stir in lemon juice and mix well. Season to taste with salt and pepper.

YOGHURT DRESSING   *2 Servings*

A tangy sauce for salads or to pour over hot dishes – very nice with cauliflower, broccoli, calabrese or carrots.

Preparation time: 5 minutes.

1 small tub/¼ pt/142ml yoghurt – low fat or Greek type,
     according to taste
1 tblsp lemon juice
½–1 tsp runny honey
Few sprigs of fresh chives or parsley

Put yoghurt into a small basin. Stir in lemon juice and honey and mix well. Mix in washed, scissor-snipped chives or parsley, and season with salt and pepper.

Yoghurt flavoured with chives is good in this recipe. A tub of plain or unsweetened yoghurt poured over salad or hot vegetables makes an instant, tasty sauce.

HUMMUS   *Serves 2*

You really need a blender or liquidiser for this recipe.

Preparation and cooking time: 10 minutes (plus soaking and cooking time if using dried chick peas, see page 76).

4 oz/100g/1 cup dried chick peas, soaked and cooked (save 1
        cup of cooking liquid) or
1 x 14 oz/435g can chick peas
2 tsp tahini (sesame cream)
1 clove of garlic, peeled and crushed, or ¼ tsp garlic powder
1 tblsp olive oil or vegetable oil
1 tblsp lemon juice
Salt, pepper

Garnish
Little extra olive oil (optional)
Few olives
Lemon chunks
Paprika pepper

To Serve
Pitta bread
Crudités (sliced raw vegetables) – carrot sticks, celery,
        cucumber, red and green peppers, etc.

Soak and cook dried chick peas, drain and save 1 cup of the liquid, or drain canned chick peas and save the liquid from the can.

Put peas in liquidiser or blender with 4 tblsp of the liquid, tahini, garlic, oil and lemon juice.

Blend for a few seconds until smooth. Taste, and season with salt and pepper, and blend again for a moment, adding more chick peas' liquid if the mixture is too stiff (it should be a thick "mayonnaise-like" paste).

Spoon in a swirl onto a serving plate. Pour a little pool of olive oil into the centre of the hummus (optional, but traditional in the Middle East) and garnish with whole olives, lemon chunks and a sprinkle of paprika pepper.

Serve with warm pitta bread and crudités, as a starter or light snack. It can also be used as a tasty accompaniment to barbecues or buffet meals.

TSATSIKI   *1–2 Servings*

One of my eldest son's specialities, after he spent the summer teaching windsurfing in Greece.

Preparation time: 10 minutes.

1 tub/¼ pt/142ml plain yoghurt – low fat or Greek style
¼ cucumber
1 clove of garlic or ¼ tsp garlic paste or ground garlic
Few sprigs of fresh mint
Handful of fresh chives
Few sprigs of fresh parsley
Salt, pepper, shake of lemon juice

Put yoghurt into a basin. Wash cucumber, cut into tiny
($\frac{1}{4}$"/$\frac{1}{2}$cm) dice and mix pieces into the yoghurt. Peel, chop
and crush fresh garlic, and mix garlic into the yoghurt
mixture. Strip mint leaves from stems, wash and chop or
scissor-snip and mix into the yoghurt, with washed, snipped
chives and parsley. Season with salt, pepper and lemon juice
to taste.

Serve with pitta bread or crudités.

CHEESE DIP   *1 generous serving*

Lovely served with crudités (see page 46) or served with
other dips at a party, to eat with crisps or savoury biscuits.

Preparation time: 5 minutes.

2 oz/50g Cheddar type cheese – choose your favourite flavour
1 oz/25g butter
2–3 tblsp milk, white wine or cider
Few drops of Worcester or tabasco sauce (optional)
Salt, pepper
Shake of cayenne pepper or paprika pepper

Grate cheese finely. Put butter into a small basin and beat
with a fork until soft. Gradually beat in the cheese and mix to
a "dip" consistency with milk, white wine or cider
(according to taste or availability!). Season with chosen
sauce, salt and pepper. Heap into a small serving dish and
garnish with a shake of cayenne or paprika pepper.

AVOCADO SAUCE OR DIP   *Serves 2*

This is a cold sauce, a very artistic shade of pale green. It makes a delicious change from mayonnaise. If making as a dip, use less yoghurt or cream, so that the dip is thicker. You can use up soft or over-ripe avocados in this recipe.

Preparation time: 5 minutes.

1 ripe (or even over-ripe) avocado pear
1 cup/5 fl oz/142ml plain yoghurt or soured cream and/or
     double cream
Few sprigs of fresh chives and/or parsley
1–2 tsp lemon juice – to taste
Salt, pepper

Peel avocado, remove stone. Chop fruit into a basin and mash well with a fork. Blend in the yoghurt or soured cream or double cream (any mixture of these, according to taste and whether you're slimming! Double cream gives an extremely rich sauce). If making a dip, just add enough yoghurt or cream to make a thick "dip" consistency.

Wash and finely scissor-snip herbs into sauce. Season to taste with lemon juice, salt and pepper.

Serve sauce with salad or as a delicious treat poured over warm green vegetables (asparagus, mange-tout peas, French beans, etc.).

WATERCRESS DIP   *Serves 1–2*

A very quick, easy to prepare dip or cold sauce, suitable as a starter or as a party dip.

Preparation time: 5 minutes.

½ cup/4 tblsp mayonnaise (see page 181)
¼ cup/2 tblsp plain yoghurt – low fat or Greek type
Small bunch of watercress
Little grated lemon rind
Paprika pepper
1 tblsp lemon juice (optional)

Mix mayonnaise and yoghurt in a small basin. Trim, wash and dry watercress, and chop or finely snip into the mixture. Stir in grated lemon rind.

Pile mixture into a small dish, and garnish with a shake of paprika.

Serve as a sauce with salad, or as a dip with crudités, pitta bread, crisps or savoury biscuits.

If the mixture is too thick for a sauce, thin it down as required with a little lemon juice.

INDEX